Joseph Brant

(Thayendanegea)

JOSEPH BRANT

(THAYENDANEGEA)

By HOWARD THOMAS

1984

NORTH COUNTRY BOOKS

18 Irving Place

Utica, NY 13501

© Prospect Books 1973

Third Printing

ISBN 0-932052-38-X

Library of Congress Catalog Card Number: 73-80132

Table of Contents

Chapter I

"I Am Thayendanegea."

THE Indian boy's paddle caught the water of the Mohawk River. The canoe leaped forward, trailing behind it a tiny whirlpool flecked with foam. The Upper Castle at Canajoharie, a straggling Mohawk settlement, passed out of view as the canoe headed up the river. The straight-backed, broad-shouldered boy who knelt in its waist had seen but eleven summers, but the muscles of his bronze body rippled with each stroke of the paddle.

His eyes scanned the shore. They shone bright and black above high cheekbones. The boy's lips formed a straight line, for laughter did not come to him easily. Gaiety rode in the single feather which seemed to grow from his scalp, but was really part of a cap that was black as his hair. It rotated slowly, as if it were joking with the serious youngster who wore it.

The boy's eyes found that something for which they had been searching. He feathered the paddle skillfully, causing the canoe to shoot toward the shore and grate on the beach. He stepped out and pulled the bark shell up on the sand.

He surveyed the canoe with pride, for he had made it with his own hands. To be sure, King Hendrick, Chief of the Upper Castle, had given him good instruction. First, they had chopped down a birch tree. It had been no easy job to strip off the bark in one piece, for one slip of the knife could mean ruin. King Hendrick had chosen ash for the gunwales and had taught the boy to curve the saplings to the proper shape. He also had helped him make the thwarts or crosspieces.

1

The boy admired with pride the wolf's head that was painted on the prow, for the boy's long-dead father, White Eagle, like King Hendrick, had been a chief of that tribe of Mohawks.

Paddle in hand, he walked into the forest, where he shinnied up a beech sapling, bent down the tip with his own weight and tied the paddle to it. When he released the tree, his paddle hung hidden high above the ground where no other boy could steal it.

The narrow trail he took into the forest smelled of fir and balsam; their needles cushioned the path for his moccasins. Bushes brushed his bare arms and legs but he did not mind.

A squirrel chattered from the branch of a sycamore. "Who are you?" it seemed to say.

"I am Thayendanegea," replied the boy. "I am the son of White Eagle, the famous warrior, who went on the great hunt to the land far to the setting sun. I never saw him, for he is in the Happy Hunting Ground."

The squirrel curled its tail up and held a nut to its mouth.

"I, too, shall be a great warrior," Thayendanegea told it. "I shall go on the warpath against the enemies of the Six Nations. I shall take many scalps. I shall be War Chief." He thumped his chest with pride.

The squirrel as it nibbled the nut, seemed to be thinking over these boastful statements. Then it did a strange and insulting thing. It turned its back, flipped its tail, and scampered up the tree. Its laughter came down from a top branch.

"Ugh!" The boy hurled a stone at his tormentor. The squirrel peeked from behind a limb. It was still chattering.

Thayendanegea stamped his feet along the path. The squirrel had asked a question and he had answered. Thayendanegea was not a name to be laughed at. It meant Bundle of Sticks, a symbol of unity. Some of the Pale Faces called him Brant's Joseph. He did not like that.

The only man who could call him Joseph was Sir William Johnson, who lived in the stone house at Fort Johnson. This Pale Face lord of the Mohawk Valley understood Indians, who called him Warraghiyagey. He always stopped to visit the boy's step-father, Nickus Brant, when he travelled up the valley. The good-natured Irishman would pat Thayendanegea on the head and tell him that some day he would be the greatest warrior of the Mohawks. Thayendanegea liked Warraghiyagey.

He left the path that led to heights overlooking the river and struck out through the undergrowth. He pushed aside some bushes and crawled into a cave whose floor was spread with pine-needles. Reaching into a niche in the wall, he took out a small pouch which contained his treasure of beads, stones and arrowheads. He tied it to his breechclout, for he would take it with him this afternoon.

This afternoon? His face lighted up. This promised to be the greatest day of his life, for King Hendrick had invited him to go with the young braves and older boys to Fort Johnson, where Sir William planned to hold a council. When Hendrick had asked him, Thayendanegea had been so excited that he hadn't uttered a word. It wasn't often that an eleven-year-old was invited to attend such an important event.

He had been asked and he would paddle down the river in his own canoe like a warrior. He would see the soldiers pass in review. He would play games with the boys and swap articles with them. He might even be able to witness the council.

He crawled out of his secret hideout and retraced his steps to the river. The squirrel chattered at him but he had no time to waste on the little pest. He walked straight to the sapling where he had hidden his paddle.

He recalled that warriors left a remembrance on a tree when they went on a journey. He was going down the river to Fort Johnson.

He took from its sheath the knife that Nickus Brant had given him. It wasn't much of a knife, for the tip had been broken and several nicks marred the blade. Carefully, he cut into the bark of the sapling what he thought resembled a canoe pointed down the river. Under it he carved a rude picture of a wolf. That was his sign. Some day, possibly many years later, he would return and find his mark on that beech. Maybe he would be a man and a warrior. He might even be a chief. The tree would grow large, but his mark would remain. As he put his knife into its sheath and stood back to admire his handiwork, his lips spread in a smile of pleasure.

He glanced at the sun, which stood almost overhead. The party planned to leave right after noon, so he would have to hurry. He climbed the sapling and retrieved his paddle.

The canoe darted down the river to the swift strokes of his paddle, while the feather rotated in the breeze. Far ahead he could see canoes in the river. He redoubled his efforts. By the time the party had reached the large island below Canajoharie, he had caught up with it.

Chapter II

"I Will Never Forget."

WHEN the Green Corn moon had hung her horn in the night sky, King Hendrick called a council of the older boys at Fort Johnson. The chief sat cross-legged before a dying fire, his back protected from the July night by a gaudy blanket, his shadow a bear against the balsams and hemlocks. Beside him sat the boy, Thayendanegea.

Whippoorwills sang serenades in the forest and lightning-bugs twinkled against the silver ribbon that was the Mohawk River. Softly across the clearing before Fort Johnson breathed the voice of the South Wind.

"The Fawn is returning to its Doe," said King Hendrick, referring to the breeze. A flash from an ember caught his face and deepened the lines which eighty summers had traced there.

The boys sat in a half circle before him. Most of them had gone through the Dream Fast, that trial of fasting and praying every Mohawk had to endure before becoming a man. A few had taken to the warpath against the French.

"There's Brant's Joseph," whispered one boy, pointing to Thayendanegea. "Why is he here? He is too young."

His neighbor shrugged.

Thayendanegea did not overhear them. He sat cross-legged beside Hendrick, hoping the chief would tell stories, for he wished to hear again the tale of Indian creation or how Hiawatha, the Onondaga chief, had combed the serpents from the hair of Atotarhoh. But he

knew that no fable, myth or story of ancient adventure
could be told during the summer months. The wood
fairies did not like idle story-telling at a time when
braves should be either on the warpath or seeking food.
They might send bees to sting the speaker's lips or cause
snakes to crawl into his bed and choke him to death.
Thayendanegea did not want such things to happen to
Hendrick.

He stole a glance at the chief, who was holding up one
hand for silence, and he knew that Hendrick meant to
talk seriously.

"The winds of eighty summers have not blown my
brains away," said Hendrick. "The Pale Face has come to
live with us. He has taught us much. We have learned but
slowly, for our hearts have not always been kind to what
our heads have told us. We have welcomed the Pale Face
to our hunting grounds, but he is like a worm that cuts
off the corn as soon as it appears. He does not wish to
live with us. He wants everything for himself. I have
been to see the White Father where the river empties
into the Great Lake. He has promised me nothing. If
Warraghiyagey cannot help us, we will be pushed farther
and farther toward the setting sun. The lands of our
fathers will be ours no more."

Night sounds crowded against the circle of Indians.
Frogs croaked in the marshlands near the river. Closer at
hand, the crickets beat upon their tiny drums. A bobcat
whined from the forest behind Fort Johnson.

"Since the days of Hiawatha," the chief went on, "the
People of the Long House have been united. We Iroquois
have been the friend of the Great White Father over the
Great Lake. Even the French Black Robes with their
tongues of oil could not make us raise our tomahawks
against him. But the Great White Father sits in his house
far away toward the rising sun. His tongue was soft when
I crossed the Great Lake to see him many summers ago,
but his chiefs are not all like Warraghiyagey. Their war
clubs are their tongues. Their promises are like a spring;

they bubble up quickly and then run away. It is only here with Warraghiyagey that the fire burns bright. Everywhere else the wood has burned and the ashes have blown away."

Sounds of merriment rose from Fort Johnson, where Sir William was entertaining officers and ladies. A mild breeze bore the sweetness of a minuet and the music of female laughter. Beyond the stone mansion rose sounds which caused Hendrick to raise a hand. He had tried to keep the traders away from this council. There was drunkenness enough at the three Mohawk villages. And now, at a time when he wished his warriors to be on their best behavior, tipsy voices sounded in the night.

"It is bad, my young brothers," he said sadly. "Fire-water is destroying our nation. We Mohawks are brave in battle. We have learned to cultivate our fields. Some of us follow the God of the Pale Face. Alas, we have learned not only the good things from our neighbors but the bad things as well. And the bad things will win unless you can wipe them out. I have fought many summers, not only on the warpath but in our castles. My days are numbered. And your days are numbered, too, unless you can learn to leave the fire-water alone."

Voices approached the circle, tipsy voices raised in song. Two warriors staggered into the group. They swayed before the dying fire. One extended a cup toward the Green Corn moon.

"Come with us, young warriors!" he cried. "We bring you joy and happiness." He wavered there, his loose lips smirking at Hendrick, his eyes wild and shiny.

Hendrick bounded up. One hand grasped the warrior's shoulder. The other held a tomahawk over his head. In tones edged with steel, he shouted, "Go, useless warrior, or I'll split your worthless head!" He twisted the brave around and threw him headlong into the fire.

A shriek rent the air. The drunken warrior, blinded with pain, struggled to his feet and wabbled toward the river, followed by his companion. A faint splash carried to Thayendanegea's ears.

Hendrick sat down, breathing heavily. It was several minutes before he spoke. "I should have killed him, but the Mohawks are a dying race, my Brothers. We have lost many braves through war and disease. We cannot afford to lose even that worthless thing." He swept the circle with his eyes. "You can make your choice, my young Brothers. If any among you would rather join the drinking, you are free to go. I have spoken."

The circle remained unbroken. Bronze statues could not have been more silent.

"I have told you about my friendship with the Great White Father over the Great Lake," said Hendrick, spreading his arms in a gesture which took in all the boys. "You have seen the evils of fire-water. You know how I feel about it. I would speak of one more thing. Thayendanegea, stand up!"

Surprised and pleased, Thayendanegea rose from his place beside the chief. He stood erect, his shoulders braced, his moccasins planted close together. He wore only a breechclout and a single feather which pointed proudly toward the Green Corn moon. In the uncertain light, his small, lithe body appeared almost white, but the narrow eyes and the high cheekbones bespoke Indian ancestry. He waited for Hendrick to speak.

"I show you Thayendanegea," said the chief. "The Pale Face calls him Brant's Joseph, but he is not the son of Nickus Brant. The boy's father was White Eagle, one of our best warriors. White Eagle left for the Happy Hunting Ground while on the great hunt to the Ohio country. Thayendanegea was born in that far country toward the setting sun. Though he has seen only eleven summers, I think he will be a famous warrior. I hope he will also be wise in council, for the Mohawks face a future that is uncertain.

"The Pale Face is driving us from our hunting grounds. He cannot be chased away by the medicine of our witch doctors. The Pale Faces are too many and the Mohawks are too few.

"Brothers, we must learn the ways of the Pale Face. We must grow better corn. We must build better houses. We must learn to talk and write like a Pale Face. If we do not choose this way, we shall be driven like snow before the freezing breath of Go-ah the Wind, and Go-ho-ne the Winter will freeze our hearts harder than the Adirondack lakes we call the Tears of God."

Hendrick struggled to his feet and placed a hand on Thayendanegea's shoulder. The boy stiffened with pride.

"You all know what Thayendanegea means," Hendrick reminded the boys. "White Eagle wanted his only son to be named Bundle of Sticks because he believed with Hiawatha that the strength of his people lay in unity. I hope this boy will remember the meaning of his name. I hope he will spend his life in keeping his people working and fighting together."

"Yo-hah! Yo-hah!" the boys shouted in approval of these words.

"The fire has burned low," said Hendrick. "Go to your rest, for tomorrow promises great things. And do not forget what I have said."

The boys rose and departed, singly and in groups.

Hendrick spoke to Thayendanegea. "You heard, Little Brother?"

The boy nodded.

"And you will remember?"

"I will never forget."

Hendrick let his hand drop from the boy's shoulder. "Go to your rest, Little Brother. May Orenda, the Great Spirit, watch over you."

Thayendanegea walked swiftly away, his single feather rising and falling with each catlike step. If he had turned around, he would have seen King Hendrick shake his head sadly.

Chapter III

"I Shall Stay"

N IGHT gave way to dawn. The sweet breath of Orenda rustled the maples. Birds stirred, tried their voices, and burst into song. The sun's tardy rays parted the clouds and slanted across the clearing to spread warmth on the stone mansion. Smoke rose from the cookhouse, where the servants were preparing breakfast. In the space between the fort and the river, Indian women crouched before fires, either blowing on embers or stirring kettles of porridge.

Thayendanegea lay curled up in a ball, a gaudy blanket wrapped around him, dreaming of the warpath. He was in the midst of a deep forest and had become separated from his party. French Indians surrounded him. His only chance lay in flight. He dodged from tree to tree but the enemy kept pace with him. At last they hemmed him in except for a narrow trail that led to a ravine. Desperate, he plunged down the path with a big Canaughwaga in pursuit. Thayendanegea, though swift of foot, had the endurance of a boy. The French Indian gained rapidly. Thayendanegea could almost smell his breath. A hand reached out and grasped his shoulder.

A blood-curdling yell broke from Thayendanegea's lips. He sat bolt upright but the hand remained on his shoulder.

"Get up, lazy one, it is already day." His sister Molly stood over him. She shook him again, saying, "Hurry, or you will miss the excitement."

He yawned, shook his head and blinked. Across the

10

hut Nickus Brant stirred, for the boy's shrill cry had destroyed the step-father's slumber. Thayendanegea saw Nickus prepare to get up, so he decided to obey Molly's command.

"Is breakfast ready?" he asked.

"Is breakfast ready?" Molly imitated his voice. "You young rascal. All you think about is your stomach."

"It is not so. I think of greater things. I am the son of White Eagle. I shall be a great warrior. I—" He closed his mouth, for Molly had left. Her laughter drifted back to him.

When he came out, his sister was watching their mother ladle porridge onto bark plates. Molly's cheeks reminded Thayendanegea of twin roses. Her hair hung over her shoulders in two braids, into which her hands were twining strips of red ribbon. Colored beads had been woven into her dress of doeskin.

The mother stared through the smoke. She spoke sharply. "Molly, stop that foolishness."

"It is not foolishness," said Molly. "I am sixteen. I must look nice today so everybody will admire me."

"Foolishness!" the mother repeated, but pride colored her tones, for no other maiden at Canajoharie could approach Molly for beauty.

Breakfast over, Thayendanegea joined the Mohawk boys at play. There was much swapping of beads, stones, knives and other articles dear to the hearts of Indian boys. They played at hunting. They raced their canoes down the river and swam in its lazy water. But they all came back promptly for dinner and the event of the afternoon, a drill by the British regulars and the militia.

Thayendanegea sat cross-legged at the edge of the paradeground, his sister beside him. He thrilled at the piercing fifes and the rat-tat-tat of the drums. He could hardly take his eyes off the young officer in scarlet and gold who rode a spirited black horse at the head of the column.

Few regulars paraded. Most of the soldiers consisted of

militiamen, some of them in makeshift uniforms, others dressed in their working clothes. They marched awkwardly. Many stumbled over their own feet.

Thayendanegea watched them sweep down the parade-ground to Fort Johnson, where Sir William stood with his higher officers to review them.

Sir William looked magnificent. His scarlet coat fitted with never a wrinkle and his breeches and waistcoat were white as snow. Thayendanegea noticed that his smiles were reserved for the ladies. When the Irishman spoke to his officers, his lips tightened into a thin line. And the boy sensed that the great man was not pleased with the review.

The young officer rode up and down the lines of awkward militiamen, urging them to greater efforts. He would dash the whole length of the parade-ground and wheel his black horse so suddenly that the animal would rise on its hind legs, pivot and charge back down the field.

Molly rose to her feet. She let out cries of joy each time the officer passed. She pressed forward. Soon she was standing alone several yards within the parade-ground.

The officer smiled and waved a hand. Molly spoke to him in words Thayendanegea could not catch. The officer laughed and continued his stunts. He completed the course and approached for a second time.

"So you want a ride," he said to Molly as he passed. "Jump up behind me the next time I come around."

Thayendanegea watched him gallop away. He also kept an eye on Molly. The girl stood poised, her cheeks flushed, her eyes shining.

The officer came down the line, laughing and joking with the Indians as he slowed down his horse.

Molly rushed forward and jumped! The officer pulled her up behind him. Away they thundered toward Sir William, with Molly's arms tightened around the officer's waist, her black hair trailing in the breeze, her face flushed with happiness.

Thayendanegea, running beside them, was soon out-distanced by the flying horse. He stopped to catch his breath and found himself beside Sir William and the officers.

"By Jove!" he heard Sir William cry. "There's a pretty picture! And a pretty girl, if I can believe my eyes!"

"You can believe them," said the officer beside him.

"Why, it's Molly Brant!" cried Sir William. "How she has grown! And what a beauty!"

Thayendanegea hurried to tell his mother the news. The horse completed the circuit. Molly, pleased and excited, rejoined them to the huzzas of the whites and the grunts of the Mohawks.

Only the mother showed displeasure. "Come, shame-less one," she said as she led her daughter away.

After the review, Sir William distributed presents con-sisting of knives, hatchets, pieces of cloth, beads and articles of clothing. To Thayendanegea went a hunting knife in a sheath, a gift which swelled his heart with pride.

"This is for my favorite warrior," Sir William had said in presenting it to him.

Thayendanegea hurried away toward the river to inspect his treasure.

Darkness had fallen before he returned. The council fire blazed against a background of hemlocks. Councils were not matters for boys of eleven, but Thayendanegea decided to see and hear all, even though Nickus Brant might punish him afterward. Clinging to the shadows, he walked on cat-feet along the edge of the clearing. A young beech spread its branches toward the fire. He crawled toward it, wound his legs around its trunk and shinned up to the overhanging limb, where he sat, back braced against the trunk, legs straddling the limb. Here he would watch. If he was to be a leader, he must know what went on in council.

The night wind chilled his shoulders, but he did not mind. Around the fire sat the important chiefs and sachems of the Mohawk nation—King Hendrick and Little Abraham and Nickus Brant. How Nickus would scold him if he found out!

Sir William and his officers came out of Fort Johnson. Sir William lighted a calumet, puffed on this pipe of peace and blew a wreath of smoke toward the Green Corn moon. The pipe was passed. Each officer, chief and sachem sucked it and puffed out a cloud of smoke. The council had begun.

King Hendrick rose, holding in his left hand a belt of white wampum, the symbol of peace. He spread his right arm in a gesture of friendship and addressed Sir William. The Mohawks were worried. Hendrick had been to New York to see the Governor, but the visit had not satisfied him. He walked across the circle and handed the belt to Sir William.

When Hendrick had returned to his place, Sir William replied in English. Daniel Claus interpreted the speech. The young German was expert in the Mohawk tongue.

Sir William regretted that Hendrick had used such loud and foul language in New York. The chief's words had shook and soiled that firm and wise covenant chain made by their wise forefathers. Sir William scolded the Mohawks for their rash behavior. He called upon them to attend a council at Onondaga, where the central fire of the Six Nations burned. In the meantime, he asked them to live at peace with their white neighbors.

The chiefs and the sachems received the speech with faces set like stone. The fire had almost burned out. The Green Corn moon cast a silvery sheen over the assemblage.

Hendrick rose. The Mohawks were not ready to accept Sir William's invitation to the council at Onondaga. They would deliberate the matter and reply on the morrow.

Thayendanegea, who had not anticipated such an abrupt end to the council, was trapped in the tree as the chiefs and sachems made ready to leave. Nickus was already striding across the clearing. His step-father would be awaiting his return.

He slid down the trunk and melted into the shadows. Crouching low, he raced along the edge of the clearing. When he reached the family shelter, his mother and Molly were seated near the fire. Nickus was standing over them.

Thayendanegea decided to put on a front. He walked toward them and said, "I am late."

Nickus slumped to his haunches and nodded to a place at his side. Thayendanegea sat down, shivering with cold and apprehension.

"Thayendanegea," said Nickus in his deliberate manner, "Warraghiyagey came to me after the review. He has brought us great honor. He has been lonely in the stone house since his wife died last year. He has asked Molly to come to the great house. Your mother and I have consented."

"Molly in the great house?" Thayendanegea could not believe his own words. He glanced at his sister.

Molly sat with head bowed, untwining the ribbon from her hair. And he noticed for the first time how pretty she was. It was no wonder Sir William wanted her for his wife.

"There is more," said Nickus. "Warraghiyagey's boy is without a playmate. His Johnny is your age. Warraghiyagey has asked for you, too."

"Me?" Thayendanegea's eyes widened.

"Yes. He wants to have you at the stone house. He wants you to learn to read and write in English. He would teach you the ways of the Pale Face."

Thayendanegea remained silent. He was a Mohawk. He wanted to hunt, to fish, to set traps, to swim in the river. He wished to become a warrior and take scalps. Hendrick had hinted that some day he might lead his people.

He also yearned for the white man's way of life. He wished to read and to write. He thought he would look splendid in scarlet and gold.

"What say you, Thayendanegea?"

The mother spoke up. "He is too young. He isn't much more than a baby."

Thayendanegea bristled. "I am not too young. I have my own canoe. I have a new knife. Warraghiyagey told me only this afternoon I was his favorite warrior."

"Foolishness," said the mother. "It is all big talk."

"And King Hendrick says I am to be a leader. I shall go on the warpath. I shall be wise in council."

"They are putting big ideas into your head. You are too young to leave home."

Nickus held up a hand. "He is young, yes, but we cannot offend Warraghiyagey. And I think we have been greatly honored. You will stay here, Thayendanegea?"

"I shall stay."

"It is well. Listen to me, Thayendanegea. The way will be long. It will not be easy. You will face disappointments."

"I know."

Nickus lighted his pipe and puffed at it. What he had to say was long in coming. "Warraghiyagey told me you should have the name of a Pale Face. To them you will be known as Joseph Brant. May Orenda watch over you, Little Brother."

Two days later, Thayendanegea stood on the shore and watched the flotilla disappear up the Mohawk River. The canoe with the wolf's head was drawn up on the beach beside him. Its paddle lay ready. All he had to do was jump into the canoe and paddle after the flotilla.

He heard Molly call to him from the stone mansion. Dinner was on the table.

He stood like a bronze image, shoulders braced, head flung back. He watched the last canoe blend with the sky before he walked toward the house. His lips trembled and he brushed a hand across his eyes.

Chapter IV

"I Am Not Afraid."

JOSEPH Thayendanegea liked Fort Johnson. From his window he could see the clearing with its many outhouses, the chapel and the mill beside the brook. Indians wandered about; sometimes they were painted for the warpath. Officers' swords flashed in the sunlight and Joseph would thrill at the sight. Some day he too might wear a scarlet coat and carry a sword.

At Fort Johnson, everyone called him Joseph. It was "Joseph, have you washed your feet?" or "Joseph, why were you late for supper?" or "Come, Joseph, it is time for your lessons." He didn't like the new name. Thayendanegea sounded like music when it rolled from the throat of a Mohawk. And it held a meaning which did not carry over to Joseph Brant. He was much upset when he learned that a brant was a little black goose. How could anyone who owned such a name become the leader of the most powerful nation in the Iroquois Confederacy?

He swallowed his pride and fell in with the routine at Fort Johnson. New things appeared each day. He was fascinated by a mirror which stretched from the floor to the ceiling of the livingroom. No matter which way he turned, this glass caught him. There were two Indian boys in the room and one could not escape the other: if he advanced, a boy just like him walked forward; if he retreated, the other Joseph moved away. It puzzled him, yet he liked to play the game.

He was performing before the mirror one afternoon

17

when Johnny Johnson caught him at it. Though Sir
William's son was the same age as Joseph, he was taller
and heavier than the Indian boy. His skin was fair and
his hair the color of straw. Now, as he stood in the
doorway watching Joseph's antics, his mouth dropped
open and a frown creased his forehead. And when
Joseph strutted across the room in imitation of a British
soldier on parade, Johnny's laugh brought him to a halt.

"Why Joseph, you silly Indian," cried Johnny.
"Haven't you ever seen a lookin' glass before?"

Joseph struggled to catch the English words. He had
studied hard at school but what did "silly" and "lookin'
glass" mean?

"Johnny, what is silly?" he asked.

Johnny hesitated. How could a boy explain such a
simple word? Everyone knew what "silly" meant.

So he said, "It's silly, that's all."

"It mean bad?" Joseph turned worried eyes on the
tow-head.

Johnny's laughter rattled against the ceiling. "No,
Joseph," he said, "it's like this." He drew circles around
his head with a finger.

Joseph thought he caught the idea. "Fire-water?" he
asked.

"No, just silly." Johnny continued to laugh.

"Ugh," grunted Joseph, angry because Johnny was
making fun of him. He decided to forget about "silly".
"And what is look in glass?" he asked, hoping to solve
his problem.

"Glass with back painted, silly." Johnny touched the
mirror. Immediately there appeared two Johnnies, both
dressed in green coat and breeches, both with yellow hair
above a pink and white face.

"Come, Joseph. You touch it."

Joseph backed away until the glass could catch him no
longer. Two Johnnies were still laughing at him.

"Oh, come on! It won't hurt you."

Joseph wasn't going to take chances with the magic

glass. It was safe to see two Josephs in a brook; he could dip a finger into the water and destroy his double. But this glass wasn't a brook.

"Are you afraid, Joseph?"

Afraid, had Johnny said? Maybe that was what "silly" meant. He feared nothing. He was to be a leader. Hendrick had told him so.

"I am not afraid," he said.

Together with that other Joseph, he touched his finger to the glass, meeting the finger of the other Joseph. With a quick movement, he tried to grasp it. Both Josephs looked puzzled.

"Lookin' glass, Joseph," Johnny explained. "It's to look at yourself in. The ladies like it. Sometimes it makes them look prettier than they are."

"Ugh," grunted Joseph. He didn't care a fig for what the ladies liked. He planned to be a warrior, not a woman.

"I silly now?" he asked Johnny.

"No, you're not silly any more," laughed Johnny, pleased that he had been able to teach Joseph.

For Sir William's son became the pupil when the boys roamed the forest. It was the Mohawk boy who taught him how to walk through the wilderness on silent feet, who showed him where chestnuts lay rich and juicy after the first frost, where the pigeons laid their eggs, where to find snow-shoe rabbits in the balsam swamps. He also taught the white boy how to shoot with the bow and arrow, how to fling the hatchet accurately, how to run with the easy lope that was the property of the Indian.

And when the salmon began to spawn, Johnny went with Joseph and the Mohawks to the mouth of their beloved river. They spent a week near the Falls of the Cohoes, where the Indians speared so many salmon that the women had to come to bring the catch home.

Here the white boy lived with the Indians for the first time, sharing their food and sleeping under the stars. And, along with the Indian boys, the old men and the women, he was allowed to spear those fish which the braves had missed.

It was at such times that Johnny thought Joseph the best boy in the world. The Mohawk lad did all things well. When he hurled the spear at a salmon, he seldom missed as Johnny did. And if the Indians held swimming races, Joseph invariably finished first, sometimes against boys two or three years older than himself. Even in gambling games, he was clever enough to take knives, beads and other articles away from the other Mohawk boys.

When Johnny came to tell his father how much he had enjoyed the trip, Sir William felt amply rewarded.

"Joseph's been happy, too," said Johnny.

Sir William raised his eyes. "Happier than he is here?"

"Yes, I think so."

"Were you happier, too?" A note of anxiety colored the father's voice. He had known white men who had chosen to live the carefree life of the Indians rather than stay in the settlements.

Johnny hesitated. "I guess I was at first," he admitted, "but I wouldn't like to live that way all the time. I guess Joseph had a better time than I did. He doesn't seem so happy since we got back."

"Hm, he'll get over it."

Sir William said this for Johnny's benefit. Joseph would never be as happy among white people. Sir William had seen much of the world. He knew that born leaders were seldom happy.

He had recognized from the start that the Mohawk boy was no ordinary lad. He was willing to admit that Joseph was brighter than his own son, that he had more courage and go-ahead than Johnny. He also knew that the Indian boy's companionship and good sense had done much to rob Johnny of the selfishness which had been his until Joseph had come to Fort Johnson.

Month by month Sir William drew Joseph closer to him. He treated him as if he were his own flesh and blood, and gave him the affection and advice that he needed during the most important years of his boyhood.

Joseph appreciated Sir William's interest. He studied hard. His English improved and he also picked up the fundamentals of mathematics. And he was ever willing to serve the man he admired. Sir William never had to speak twice. Joseph went out of his way to please him, thus cementing a friendship which was honest and sincere.

Chapter V

"My Place Is with My People."

TWO years passed. When the leaf of the dogwood was the size of a squirrel's ear, Sir William called a war council of the Iroquois.

For Joseph, this event was charged with excitement. Indans of the Six Nations were arriving at Fort Johnson each day. Their bodies were painted brilliantly and their tomahawks flashed in the sunlight. The Mohawks came first and camped near the stone mansion. The Oneidas, the Cayugas, the Onondagas and the Tuscaroras soon joined them. The distant Senecas, led by their chiefs, completed the gathering. From Fort Johnson to the Mohawk River, the sloping ground was dotted with shelters. When evening fell, hundreds of fires pushed aside the darkness.

Joseph, standing in the livingroom of the mansion, could see warriors wandering to and fro, their greased bodies glistening, their feathers waving with each step. And his mind was troubled. Though he was dressed in the English manner, he wished to strip to the skin and paint his body red and black. After all, he was a Mohawk. His people were taking to the warpath and he longed to go with them.

Sir William opened the council with a long speech in which he told of the arrival of General Braddock, who was to protect the Indians against the French. His talk was filled with expressions the Indians understood and loved. "The tree," he said, referring to himself, "which you have so often and so earnestly hoped might be again

22

set up, is now raised and fixed in the earth by so powerful a hand that its roots will take a firm and deep footing. Its branches will be a comfortable shade for you and all your allies to take shelter under.

"By this belt I now invite you and all your allies to come and sit under this tree. Here you may freely open your hearts and get all your wounds healed.

"I do, Brethren, at the same time, remove the embers which remain at Albany, where the council was held last year. I rekindle the fire of council and friendship at this place. And this fire I shall make of such wood as will give the clearest light and the greatest warmth. I hope it will prove comfortable and useful to all such as will come and light their pipes at it. May it dazzle and scorch all those who are or may be enemies to it."

Red Head replied to Sir William on the second day. "The Six Nations have long been in darkness," said the Onondaga chief. "They are now extremely obliged to the King, their Father, for restoring to them that clear and comfortable light which in old times cheered their forefathers.

"The fire at Albany last year was so low and so bad that they could not even find a spark with which to light a pipe. The fire you kindle here, as well as that at Onondaga, they will cherish. All other fires they thus kick away as unnatural and hateful."

Here Red Head gave a violent kick, thus putting out the imaginary fire which had caused them so much unhappiness.

He advanced to where Sir William sat. In his hand lay a belt of purple wampum bordered with red, the symbol of war. He handed the belt to Sir William, bowed three times, and returned to his place.

Sir William accepted the challenge to war. "The Indians of the South are joining General Braddock," he cried. "Set them an example. If you desire to treat me as a brother, go with me. My war-kettle is on the fire! My canoe is ready to put into the water! My gun is loaded!

My sword is at my side! My axe is sharpened!" He rose
to his feet and threw down the war belt in General
Braddock's name.

It was picked up by an Oneida sachem. An interpreter
started the war dance. The sachems joined in the chorus.
A tub of punch was dragged from the stone mansion.
The Indians drank Sir William's health far into the night.

Braddock's campaign ended in failure and the general
lost his life in the Pennsylvania wilderness. Sir William,
hoping to keep the Mohawk Valley for his King, planned
to attack the French near Lake Champlain.

Johnny was happy, for his father had promised to
take him on this expedition. Johnny, an overgrown
youngster of thirteen, took pleasure in bothering Joseph.

"How do you like me?" he asked as he strutted in a
scarlet coat. "Don't you wish you had a uniform and
could go with us?"

Joseph wanted to go to war, but he held his tongue.
Previous taunts had led to arguments; though he was
smaller than Johnny, a few wrestling bouts had left
young Johnson flat on his back.

"I have a sword, too," Johnny boasted, "and a new
hat with gold braid. I shall be a real soldier. I'll tell you
all about it when I get back."

Joseph grunted and turned away. Johnny's face crim-
soned at the insult.

"Why, you poor Indian," he cried. "You know
nothing about war. You can keep your nose stuck in a
book while I go out and kill the Frenchies. You can stay
here with the women."

It was Joseph's turn to flush. He who was destined to
wear King Hendrick's mantle was being called a woman,
just as if he were a Delaware and not a Mohawk. He
wheeled and rushed Johnny. The white boy landed in a
corner. His face became redder than the new coat which
he had worn so proudly.

A hearty laugh sounded from the doorway. Sir William
stood there. His hands held his stomach, which bounced

up and down with each joyful sound that came from his mouth.

"Sure and you fetched the lad a good one, Joseph," he called to the Indian boy. "And you deserved it well, my fine bucko," he told Johnny. "If you can't keep a civil tongue in your head and insist on thinking with your breeches, that's where you should land. And if you keep on thinking that way, you'll get nowhere fast. Come, stand up on your feet, my lad."

Johnny obeyed, slowly, sulkily.

"Don't take it ill, Johnny," said his father. "The trouble is, you didn't pick on the right man. Joseph can't be trifled with. You should have found that out by now. So come, shake his hand and call it quits."

"I not mean to throw him so hard," the Mohawk boy apologized, "but I not like him call me woman."

Johnny grinned sheepishly. "I'm sorry, Joseph," he said, shaking hands. "I let my tongue get too long." He looked up at Sir William. "Father, why don't you buy Joseph a uniform and let him come along with us?"

Joseph walked to the window. He had heard the request. It was sporting of Johnny, especially after the roughing the white boy had received. He thrilled with the thought of wearing British scarlet, but the moment he saw the painted warriors he knew that his place was among them. There would be no scarlet coat for him. He wanted to go to war as an Indian.

Sir William did not answer Johnny's question right away. Instead, he strode over to the window and placed a hand on Joseph's shoulder. Together they watched the Indians moving around between the house and the river. Sir William read the boy's thoughts. Many a time he had wished that he too were an Indian. Often in the old days he had appeared at their celebrations painted and feathered in the Mohawk manner.

"What do you say, Thayendanegea?" he asked, choosing the boy's Indian name deliberately.

The Mohawk lad continued to stare at the scene outside. Several moments passed before he replied, "I like to go, Warraghiyagey, but my place is with my people. Red coat is fine for Johnny but not for me."

"Well answered, my boy. You shall ask Hendrick for his permission. I'm sure he'll let you come with us—as a Mohawk."

Joseph ran to his room and stripped off the English clothes. A few moments later he rushed out of the stone mansion. He wore breechclout and moccasins. A solitary feather grew from his scalp. It twirled in the breeze as he raced across the clearing in search of King Hendrick.

Chapter VI

"King Hendrick—Dead!"

JOHNNY Johnson rolled over and kicked with his feet. "Boy, but this water feels great!" he cried.

Joseph took a shallow dive and came up beside his friend. "Ugh!" he gasped, shaking his head to prevent ear-bubbles.

"I wish I could stay in all morning, Joseph. I'd rather swim than dress up and watch my father name a lake." Johnny swam away.

"We better go in, Johnny. Your father be mad as wet hen if you late for parade."

"I suppose you're right," grumbled young Johnson. "But what does it matter if this lake is called Lac St. Sacrament or Lake George? The water will never know the difference." He dog-paddled slowly toward shore.

"Beat you in!" came Joseph's challenge.

Johnny's arms flailed at the water. He was a strong swimmer but not a speedy one. Out of the corner of his eye he saw the Indian boy come abreast and pass him. When he arrived on the beach, Joseph was jumping up and down, flipping the drops off his body.

"I'll challenge you to a long race some of these days," said Johnny, "and then you won't win so easy."

Joseph slipped into his breechclout, his sole article of clothing, and placed on his head the cap with its rotating feather. He watched Johnny don the many garments needed by a Pale Face and was glad he had come to war as an Indian. He never understood why the Pale Face tried so hard to be uncomfortable in summer.

Johnny read his thoughts. "I'd run around naked the way you do, Joseph, if Father would let me. But when I complain he always laughs at me and asks me if I want to become an Indian."

The Mohawk boy said nothing. He was proud to be an Indian.

The camp stirred with activity. Troops were arriving daily. Ships were needed to transport them up the lake. Axes rang in the forest. Tall trees crashed to the ground. The tapping of hundreds of hammers echoed across the lake. Keel after keel cut the blue waters. Wagons rumbled into camp, loaded with ammunition and guns; their teamsters cursed at straining oxen. Haste was necessary, for scouts had reported that Baron Dieskau with his French, Canadians and Indians was preparing to attack Fort Edward.

A bugle sounded. The men dropped their tools and ran toward the shore. A procession was approaching the lake, guided by fifes and drums. It was a brilliant display of scarlet and gold, led by Sir William on a white horse.

Johnny slipped on his second shoe. "We might as well watch from here," he remarked. "I'll hear about his later."

Sir William rode into the lake until the water covered the horse's fetlocks. While the fifes shrilled and the drums played rat-tat-tat, the Irishman unfurled a British flag and held it aloft. The music ceased. In a loud voice Sir William shouted, "I name these waters Lake George, not only in honor of his Majesty but to make sure of his dominion here." Thunderous cheers drowned the fifes and drums.

Joseph watched the ceremony without twitching a muscle. And, as usual, he was filled with admiration for Sir William. The Mohawks loved pomp and ceremony. There was much ritual to their dances and their councils. But Warraghiyagey could outdo them every time.

His attention was drawn from Sir William by a shout from the forest. Four Mohawks were racing toward the shore. At their head ran Paulus, son of King Hendrick. Joseph, hurrying forward, saw Sir William ride to meet the messengers.

Paulus was winded. He had run far. "French—coming!" he gasped. "They many. They got more Indians than us. They only few miles away."

"Well spoken, Paulus," said Sir William. He turned to young Daniel Claus. "Order scouts into the forest! Send messengers to Albany for re-enforcements."

That night there was feverish activity in camp. The forest rang anew with the thud of axes. Trees toppled to the ground and were hauled into place to form a breastwork. The Mohawks danced before their fires, their bodies decorated with stripes of red and black.

To Joseph Thayendanegea it was a night to remember. He covered his body with a coat of grease, over which he daubed black paint slashed with stripes of red. From his neck to his scalplock, one side of his face was a bright carmine; the other side remained unpainted. Around each eye he traced circles of black, according to the Mohawk custom.

His tomahawk had been sharpened days before. He drew a finger across the edge to test its keenness. His knife rested in its sheath. It would be ready should a scalping fall his way.

He was proud of his appearance. He loved his Indian weapons. But above all, he cherished the rifle which Sir William had given him the day they left Fort Johnson. It was bright and shiny, smooth to the touch, easy against his shoulder. He understood why the Mohawks liked rifles better than tomahawks. Rifles were one advance in civilization which they were able to appreciate.

Sir William held a council at dawn, and outlined his plan of battle. One thousand troops and two hundred Indians were to interrupt the French while the main army remained behind the breastwork. Colonel Ephraim Williams, a dour New Englander, was to command this expedition. Hendrick would be in charge of the Indians.

Sir William described his plan with confidence. He did not expect opposition in council.

King Hendrick sat wrapped in his blanket, the boy Joseph Thayendanegea at his side. The chief's leathery face showed his disapproval, but he did not speak until Sir William asked his opinion.

"The French have many Indians," replied Hendrick. "We have only two hundred. If we are to fight, we are too few; if we are to be killed, we are too many."

Sir William's face reddened. His jaws set. He did not deny Hendrick's blunt statement. It was all too true. He continued with his plan of action. The force was to be divided into three parties. Williams nodded approval, but Hendrick merely grunted.

"What say you, Hendrick?" asked Sir William.

The old chief picked up three sticks from the ground. "Put these sticks together," he answered, "and you cannot break them. Take them one by one and you will do it easily." He broke the sticks one by one and tossed them aside. "United we will win; divided we will fall. Stand up, Thayendanegea!"

The boy obeyed.

"The Mohawks know what Thayendanegea means. You know, Warraghiyagey. To our Pale Face brothers I say, Thayendanegea means a Bundle of Sticks. It means more than mere sticks. It means we are a strong united people. We would go on the warpath together. If we must die, we wish to die together."

Hendrick had said his last word in council. It was ignored. Sir William clung to his plan, but he made one last show of friendship to the chief who had been his right arm for fifteen years. Hendrick was heavy on his feet. He could not move swiftly enough to lead his warriors. To him Johnson gave his own horse.

The three columns moved into the forest. King Hendrick rode at the head of the Mohawks. His painted body looked fat and heavy, but his feathers waved proudly over his head. Joseph Thayendanegea ran at the side of the horse.

Baron Dieskau, the French commander, anticipating the British move, had formed an ambuscade in the shape of a crescent, with Indians and Canadians on the wings and the French regulars in the center. Colonel Williams, who had neglected to send out skirmishers, ordered an advance. Hendrick rode toward the ambush, followed by his warriors.

The crack of a musket broke the stillness. King Hendrick put a hand to his head. His body toppled forward on the horse's neck, then slid to the ground with a sickening thud. He lay on his back, a thread of blood trickling from his temple. The horse, frightened, bolted down the forest path.

Joseph stood there, stunned, bewildered. Scalp yells rang through the forest. The pat-pat of musketry sounded all around him. The Mohawks were racing from tree to tree, trying to avoid the deadly fire of the unseen enemy. Yet he did not move.

A hand pushed him roughly. It was Paulus telling him to seek shelter. Hendrick was dead. Nothing could be done for him. Joseph staggered into the forest. He felt weak and helpless. Strange lights danced before his eyes. He grasped the trunk of a sapling to keep from falling, and leaned his forehead against the cool bark.

The Mohawks were fighting for their lives. Several braves had been killed with Hendrick in the surprise attack. Others were making their way from tree to tree. These men pressed hands to bullet wounds. The New Englanders also had been caught. The crack-crack of their rifles could be heard through the cries of the Indians.

A bullet whistled over Joseph's head and buried itself in the sapling. He came to his senses with a start. Through the smoke he could see a Canaughwaga sliding from tree to tree. The French Indian moved rapidly, his knife between his teeth, his tomahawk raised. His eyes glistened like those of a rattlesnake ready to strike. He reached the spot where Hendrick lay. The knife was in his hand. The scalp yell rose to his lips.

Joseph raised the rifle to his shoulder and drew a bead on the Canaughwaga warrior. The rifle barked. Its kick knocked Joseph down.

The Canaughwaga leaped high in the air. The knife dropped from nerveless fingers. He crashed to the ground, quivered, and lay still.

Joseph patted his smoking rifle. It had served him well. But there was more work to be done. He crouched low, his tomahawk grasped firmly in his right hand, his knife between clenched teeth. A gleam of anticipation lighted his face. At thirteen he was to take his first scalp.

He found the Canaughwaga a few feet from Hendrick's body. The French Indian lay dead, shot through the head. Joseph knelt over his victim. His knife entered at the forehead and made an incision around the scalp. This done, he grasped the scalplock in his right hand and pulled with all his strength. He yelled in triumph as he held the prize high above his head.

His body stiffened. The breath of Orenda carried the Mohawk call to retreat.

"Oo-nah! Oo-nah!"

He tied the scalp to his belt with trembling fingers. His thoughts were now of Hendrick. If the chief lay there, he would surely be scalped. That would be an everlasting disgrace to the Mohawk nation.

The boy acted quickly. He grasped Hendrick's body by the shoulders and tugged. Hendrick was heavy. His body moved only a few inches. Yet Joseph toiled on. Inch by inch, he drew the body of the chief into the bushes beside the path. Having accomplished this, he bounded down the path toward the British camp. All around him men were hurrying toward the breastwork. Some were limping painfully, others were helping comrades. He reached the breastwork. A hand pulled him over the top. He lay on the ground, panting.

It was Johnny who came to him.

"Joseph!" he exclaimed. "Are you hurt?"

"No—just out of wind."

"What has happened?"

"Ambushed, Johnny! King Hendrick—dead! Many others—dead! French—coming!"

"I'll tell Father." Johnny left on the run.

The French waited a quarter of an hour before attacking the breastwork. Joseph could see them at the edge of the forest. He could hear the Canaughwaga scalp yells as the French Indians searched for victims. He was glad he had hidden Hendrick's body. He felt sure no French Indian would take the Mohawk chief's scalp.

The French regulars advanced from the forest. Their white uniforms offered excellent targets for the Yankee squirrel-hunters. They advanced by platoons, steadily, without flinching, though gaps were bored in their ranks by balls from Sir William's cannon. They tried first the left and then the right, but the breastwork was not to be taken. At last they retreated to the woods, leaving the field strewn with white-clad figures.

The victory lay with Sir William, but the Irishman was not around at the finish. He had caught a bullet in his hip and had been taken to his tent, much to his disgust. He carried the bullet with him the rest of his life.

The Mohawks, who had lost not only their leader but forty of their warriors, were low in spirit. Their anger also had been kindled because Sir William had refused to turn over to them Baron Dieskau, the defeated French general, who lay desperately wounded within the British camp. Paulus was filled with a spirit of revenge. At the funeral of Hendrick and the other warriors on the following day, the son of the Mohawk leader pounded his chest and cried, "My father is not dead! He will always live! I will avenge him!"

Three days later the Mohawks took the trail to the Mohawk Valley to thaw out their cold hearts over their dead. Joseph went with them, wearing a scalp at his belt. He walked with head held erect, but his heart lay like a stone; for he, of all the Mohawks, probably had loved Hendrick the most. Young though he was, he realized that something had been taken away from his nation, something sturdy and fine, something which would be hard to replace. Hendrick had been every inch a king.

"Hendrick, my Chief," he muttered, "May the spirit of Orenda watch over you."

Chapter VII

"I Would Sleep Now."

JOSEPH attended the ceremonies at Canajoharie in honor of Hendrick and his warriors. There was much wailing by the women and too much drinking among the men. The Albany traders came with solemn faces and kegs of rum. Night after night the forest rang with the cries of tipsy warriors. The sachems were helpless to stop them.

It took the hunting season to do that. No Iroquois went after game without making full preparations. First, all human odors had to be driven from his body; second, weapons and food had to be made ready for the trip to the forest.

Joseph sat on his haunches sharpening his knife. For several days he had not eaten any foods which might have a conspicuous odor. Purges had cleansed his system. And only yesterday he had sat for hours in a sweat lodge while all the poisons oozed from his pores. An odor of sweet ferns lingered from the rubdown that had followed this steam bath.

He held his knife to the light, the better to examine the length of its blade. He smiled as he traced its edge with a brown finger. In his mind he checked over the articles he had prepared for the hunt—dried corn and pemmican, an extra pair of moccasins, a blanket, a bow and a quiver filled with arrows. And close at hand stood his rifle, newly-cleaned, with a powder horn beside it. He placed the knife in its sheath. He was ready for the hunt.

The hunting party crossed the Mohawk and tramped

all day through the forest north of Canajoharie. Toward
dusk scouts were sent out. On their return, a ceremonial
dance was performed. The pipe was passed and each
hunter took a pull and blew smoke into the air. Joseph,
being the youngest of the party, received the pipe last.
He touched its stem to his lips, puffed a cloud of smoke
and breathed a silent prayer in which he asked the Great
Spirit for his favor in the hunt.

Next morning at the crack of dawn the party divided.
Some were to drive the deer. Others waited beside the
runways the animals used in their search for food, salt
and water. Nickus Brant, being a chief, was given a
position on the most important runway. Joseph knelt
beside him.

The boy knew the rules. He was to keep quiet, avoid
talking, eat no bark or think a song, for deer loved music.
If a hunter even thought a song, the deer would know he
was there.

The breath of Ga-oh caused the leaves to drop around
him. Soon the spirit of the wind would be walking his
freezing way, whispering frosts on his breath. And Go-
ho-ne, the winter, would lay his hand upon the land and
harden it still as rocks.

Go-ho-ne would say, "I am powerful and strong. I
send the North Wind to blow all over the earth and its
waters stop to listen to his voice as he freezes them
asleep. When I touch the sky, the snow hurries down and
the hunters hide by their lodge fire. The birds fly scared
and animals creep into their caves."

Joseph did not hate Go-ho-ne. It was fun to play in
the snow and to slide along the icy Mohawk. He didn't
mind cracking holes in the ice to take a plunge in the
cold waters. And winter was the season for story-telling.
While the North Wind howled around the bark houses
like a bear prowling in the sky, groups would sit on their
haunches around the fires and listen to tales of the
Iroquois: the story of creation; how Hiawatha combed
the snakes of war from the hair of the rival chief,

Atotarhoh; how the tribes of the Mohawks became united.

Such thoughts made him sad, for Hendrick had been the greatest of story-tellers. He looked at Nickus Brant, wrapped tightly in a gay blanket. No, Nickus the silent one could not weave yarns, nor could any of the other chiefs at the Upper Castle. Hendrick would be missed this winter.

They waited two days without seeing a deer, but on the third morning sounds from the north caused Nickus to crouch low and grasp his rifle with sure fingers. Joseph imitated his step-father. And, sure enough, down the runway bounded three deer, two of them bucks.

"Take the second one," whispered Nickus.

Joseph had been on the warpath. He had lifted a scalp. But now, with the beautiful animals moving toward him, a wave of hotness swept over the boy, though his hands were cold and shaking. The sound of Nickus' gun brought him to his senses. He too aimed and fired.

The leading buck crashed into the forest, followed by the doe. The other buck staggered down the runway and collapsed at Joseph's feet.

"Ugh," grunted Nickus, kneeling at the side of the fallen animal. The deer's eyes were glazing. Though the boy had shot the deer, it was an unwritten law of the Mohawks that if two of a party shot at a deer, the older was always to take credit for the killing. With swift, accurate strokes, Nickus peeled back the hide and cut off the hot meat in strips. Together, they would carry the slabs of flesh back to camp for drying.

The hunt lasted a fortnight. The hunters plodded home, each carrying baskets filled with venison. Nickus and Joseph crossed the river and stopped at the edge of the village, where they hid their baskets in the hollow of a dead elm tree, for if any Mohawk left game within the limits of the village, it would become the property of his whole tribe.

Once they reached the bark house, Nickus whispered to his wife. She went to the hollow tree to bring in the baskets of venison, while the hunters stuffed themselves with the food she had prepared for them.

"I would sleep now," said the boy, rising.

His mother entered the hut in time to hear his words. She held up her hand.

Joseph slumped to his haunches.

"Warraghiyagey is back," she said. "He wants you to come to him."

He frowned. He had expected Sir William's message.

"When?"

"Tomorrow."

"I shall go."

"It is well," said Nickus Brant. "Sleep now. You are tired."

Joseph rose at dawn. His mother had breakfast ready. The boy ate without comment. For the second time he was leaving Canajoharie. On that earlier occasion he had been happy. Today the parting was more difficult. For four months he had lived the carefree life of a Mohawk. The deerskin trousers and hunting shirt were more comfortable than Pale Face clothing. The moccasins he would keep, to be sure. He could never suffer the torture of shoes.

He fingered the dried scalp at his belt. He was proud of that trophy. It had won him the praise of the Mohawk warriors. Would it fit into the Pale Face's way of life? Warraghiyagey did not approve of scalping. He called it barbarism. Joseph took the scalp from his belt and handed it to his mother.

He arrived at Fort Johnson by noon. Molly met him at the door. In her arms lay a tiny infant.

"Welcome, Little Brother," she said in Mohawk. "You have been a long time away." Molly smiled at him, showing her excellent teeth. "See?" She pulled the blanket away from the baby's face. "Isn't he a fine boy?"

"Ugh!" Joseph wasn't curious about babies.

"Warraghiyagey is proud of him," boasted Molly. "Isn't he handsome?"

Joseph grunted again. "He's all right."

This answer did not satisfy Molly. "I shall tell Warraghiyagey you don't like our baby," she pouted.

"I didn't say that."

"But you didn't say he was beautiful," cooed the mother, kissing the baby's forehead.

"All right, he's beautiful. And I'm hungry."

"I've never seen a boy like you. Always hungry. Very well, dinner is almost ready. Go to your room and change into civilized clothes. And wash your hands and face, by all means."

"Molly," asked the boy, "did you know I took a scalp at Lake George?"

Molly had heard Johnny tell about Joseph's adventure, but she wanted to hear about it from her brother's lips. So she asked, "You did? Tell me about it."

Joseph told his story in the best Indian manner, filling it with metaphors and descriptive adjectives.

Molly did not move a muscle. She might be the lady of the great house, but she had not lost her interest in the warpath. At the close she said, "Good, Joseph. You are a real warrior now. Let me see the scalp."

"I left it with Mother."

"But why? You should be proud to wear it."

"Warraghiyagey would not like it."

Molly did not argue. "Hurry and get washed and changed," she told her brother.

Chapter VIII

"I Shall Lead My People!"

SIXTEEN moons passed. Joseph, almost fifteen years old, prepared for the Dream Fast. Silently and alone, he climbed the heights behind Fort Johnson and walked into the forest. Though the trail was edged with snow, he wore only a breechclout and moccasins. But he did not feel cold, for his heart was warmed by the thought that he would return from the forest a man and a warrior.

Joseph had grown by leaps and bounds. As he loped along the narrow path, the muscles of his well-knit body rippled with each graceful stride. Low-hanging limbs brushed against his shoulders and berry bushes clutched at his legs with sharp fingers, but he paid no attention to the bite of their thorns. At sundown he stood, miles away from Fort Johnson, on a hill from which he could see the winding Mohawk River.

With his tomahawk and knife, he built a leanto. He did this by bending down saplings and fastening their ends to pegs in the ground. Over them he placed boughs and leaves to keep the rain out. Clever use of flint and twigs brought the warmth of a fire.

A few yards away a spring bubbled up through the snow. He stretched full length on the ground and drank his fill of the water, which stilled his hunger and thirst. Returning to his fire, he lay down on the pine needles and fell asleep.

The breath of dawn blew across the dead fire and chilled his body which was curled up into a ball. He shivered. His hand reached out to pull back the bed cover. It found only pine needles.

He woke with a start, conscious that he was alone in the forest, that his body was cold as ice. He rolled out of his leanto and jumped to his feet. For several minutes he danced around, slapping his arms across his chest to bring back circulation.

A whirring in the underbrush told him that a partridge had been disturbed by his gymnastics. A gray squirrel, watching him curiously, chattered defiantly and scampered up a tree. Under ordinary circumstances Joseph might have tried to make friends with the gray gossip that now peeked out at him from behind the trunk.

Today he had more important things to do. Once circulation had been restored to his arms and legs, he climbed to the spot overlooking the valley. The sun was creeping above a bank of clouds. He spread his arms toward it. Throwing back his head, he cried:

"Oh, Great Spirit, look down upon me.
Grant me a sign of thy favor.
I would be a true son of the Wolf.
I would be a warrior among warriors.
Hear me, Orenda, and give me the sign!"

Silence was the answer, the silence of the primeval forest, the winding river and the Adirondack Lakes which the Mohawks called the Tears of God. It was a beautiful silence, undisturbed by those sounds which he connected with human beings. He stood there, alone, unafraid, his arms stretched toward the reddening east, his eyes fastened upon the ball that represented the Great Spirit, his lips parted by the awe which the opening of the day had impressed upon his mind.

Realization came that he was not ready to receive a sign from the Great Spirit. His arms lowered and his head bowed before that Something which was greater than any human being. He turned away and walked back to his leanto. He was no longer cold.

For five days and nights no food crossed his lips; no blanket covered his shoulders. The sweet water was his only nourishment. And each dawn he walked to the heights and repeated his plea.

On the fifth morning the East Wind spread its breath like a Moose and drew a blanket of clouds over the sun's face. Rain dampened the boy's shoulders, but he did not give up, though he was so weak that it was difficult for him to raise his arms toward the Great Spirit.

Once back into his leanto, he crouched before a fire which sputtered against the attacks of the wind and the rain. His thoughts drifted to the story Hendrick often had told.

Long ago another boy had gone on the Dream Fast. He had endured the hardships. He had prayed to the Great Spirit. For ten days and ten nights he had watched for the sign, but no sign had come. The warriors, hearing no word from him, had come in search of him. They had found him dead beside the embers.

Joseph shuddered. Other boys had quit when no sign had come. They had gone home to become mere clods who could never take to the warpath and be successful. A dull pain clutched at his stomach. He no longer wanted water from the spring. His head felt light, but his body had no life. He dropped into a heavy sleep.

How long he was lost to the world, he did not know. He was awakened by a cry from the forest. He struggled to his feet and placed a hand on a sapling to lend him support. Into his dulled brain crept the full meaning of that cry.

It was the call of a wolf!

He stood with his body resting against the sapling. The days of fasting had taken their toil. The skin stretched tightly across his cheekbones and his eyes were set in hollows. He could see his heart pound as if it were trying to burst its way between his ribs. And there was no strength left in his legs. They did not even seem to be a part of him.

The only thing that remained alive was his spirit. Through the long days of fasting and disappointments, he had never lost faith in himself. He had always felt that the sign would come. He knew he would not be overlooked by Orenda, the Great Spirit.

And now the wolf had called to him!

The cry in the dawn was the sign for which he had been waiting. It meant that he was ready to become a member of the Wolf tribe of the Mohawks. He must answer that cry!

But how? If he let go of the sapling he would merely sink to the ground. He would be found there, dead. And all of his trials would be as a passing wind.

No, he would not die in the wilderness. He would gain the heights. He would offer his thanks to the Great Spirit!

He gave up his hold on the sapling and took a step forward. His leg held no life. It gave way under his weight, and he sprawled headlong in the path.

But he refused to lie there. Slowly, but painfully, he dragged his body along the ground. Using his elbows, he managed to edge himself along a foot at a time. Now and then a stone in the path or the trunk of a tree would help his progress, though his fingers hardly had strength enough to grasp them. But he kept moving along, though he stopped every few minutes to rest.

The ground began to rise, thus increasing his difficulties. But with it rose his spirit and that could not be conquered. His elbows and fingers bled from scratches and bruises. His legs were marked by stones over which he had dragged them. His breath came in sobs. He bit his lip to keep back the tears. A foot! Another foot! Would he never reach the top?

A cool breeze caressed his tired and bleeding body. It was the breath of Go-hay, the Spring. She was letting the breezes blow her long hair to the clouds. Soon she would send down gentle rains that whispered to the grass to grow.

Joseph, hearing Go-hay's voice, felt rise within him a new strength. His knees helped his elbows after the last rise. He was atop the ridge at last!

The sun was sending its first rays across his beloved valley. Birds sang from the branches of the beeches and birches and squirrels chattered a welcome.

Joseph had been near death. That he knew. For only last night he had dreamed of eating strawberries, and strawberries always grew on the trail to the Happy Hunting Ground.

He was alive. All around him nature was calling. The red ball that was the Great Spirit was warming his shoulders and Go-hay the Spring was whispering in his ears.

He struggled to his feet and stretched his arms toward the east. A whisper came from his parched lips:

"Oh, Great Spirit, I thank thee.
I have waited long for thy sign
It has come at last.
I have heard the cry of the Wolf!
I shall be a great warrior!
I shall lead my people!"

All his strength went into this prayer. His knees buckled and he sank to the earth. He lay as if dead.

It was Johnny Johnson who found him. The white boy had been upset over his absence. Each morning he had pleaded with his father to send a rescue party after him. But Sir William, who knew the Indians better than Johnny did, would not consent. When five days and five nights had passed and Joseph had not returned, Johnny could wait no longer.

He knew where Joseph was going, for the Mohawk lad often had told him where he would meet the Great Spirit. So he followed the trail into the forest, taking with him an Indian from Fort Johnson.

Together, they made a stretcher of saplings and brought Joseph home.

For a day and a night the Mohawk boy lay as if dead. But, in less than a week he was up on his feet again, a warrior ready to take to the warpath.

Chapter IX

"You Will Make a Pale Face Out of Me."

SOON after Joseph's nineteenth birthday, war broke out again.

Fort Niagara commanded the carrying place between Lake Erie and Lake Ontario. Through this fort poured the furs which the French traders got from the Indians at Fond du Lac and Green Bay. As long as the French held Fort Niagara, the wealth of the West was being directed to Quebec rather than to Albany.

General Prideaux, with an army of British regulars, undertook the job of taking Fort Niagara from the French. Sir William Johnson served as second in command. Joseph and seven hundred Indians went along. Prideaux was killed during the siege of the fort, but Sir William carried on the attack with such skill and daring that Niagara fell to the British.

Joseph also took part in Lord Geoffrey Amherst's capture of Montreal, an achievement which crushed the hopes of a French empire in the new world.

Joseph liked the warpath. He fought well. He kept his head when the going proved difficult. The Mohawks, since the death of Hendrick, had lacked leadership. Little Abraham of the Lower Castle at Fort Hunter, the War Chief, preferred the Christian religion to fighting battles. On the other hand, Joseph Brant, warrior, was fearless in battle and cool in council. More and more the Mohawks began to turn to the son of White Eagle for leadership.

After the campaigns against Fort Niagara and Montreal, Joseph returned to Fort Johnson. It seemed the

natural thing for him to do, for the stone mansion had
been his home for eight years.

The Mohawks at Canajoharie voiced their displeasure.
They wanted him to remain with them, to marry some
Indian girl, and to aid them in council and on the
warpath. They claimed that Sir William was trying to
make a Pale Face out of the son of White Eagle.

When Joseph went to Sir William to talk over the
situation, he found his friend entertaining two Indians in
the livingroom at Fort Johnson. Joseph recognized Sam-
son Occum, a preacher whom he had met before.
Occum's companion was a young Delaware.

"Come in, Joseph," said Sir William. "You remember
Mr. Occum? He was here last year."

Joseph shook hands with Occum, a thick-set Indian
about forty years of age.

"And this young man is David Fowler," added Sir
William. "David, may I present Joseph Brant? He is
Molly's brother. Joseph has been with us eight years. He
fought bravely at Niagara. He is one of the lads I've been
talking about."

David Fowler rose. The Delaware's English clothes
hung loosely over his slight body. His cheekbones bulged
prominently beneath burning eyes. He wore his hair in
the English manner.

"I am pleased to meet you, Joseph," he said in English. "Sir William has said many fine things about you."

Joseph's face lighted up. He spoke to Fowler, but he
directed his words at Sir William. "I am glad," he said.

"Sit down, Joseph," Sir William said. "These men
come from Dr. Eleazer Wheelock's school at Lebanon in
Connecticut. Dr. Wheelock educates Indians. Mr. Occum
was his first pupil and David has just graduated from the
school."

Joseph's face became a mask. He had not come to talk
about schools. True, Johnny Johnson was studying in
Philadelphia. That was all right for Sir William's heir. He
was a white boy. He would be a wealthy man. But for
Joseph, more important things loomed on the horizon.

"Mr. Fowler came here to see some of our young men," Sir William went on. "He would like to talk with you, Joseph."

"Yes, Joseph," said Fowler, "Sir William has spoken so well of you that I would like to encourage you to come with me to Connecticut. Would you like to go to Dr. Wheelock's school?" The Delaware's face glowed with enthusiasm.

"I would like to speak to Sir William first," replied the Mohawk.

"We'll leave you," said Occum. "I'll show David how well you are situated here, Sir William."

The two visitors rose. They bowed to Sir William before leaving.

"Well, Joseph, what's troubling you?" asked Sir William, a smile playing at the corners of his mouth, "Are you in love?"

Joseph was in no mood for humor. "No," he answered, rather abruptly.

"Then what is biting you?"

"It is nothing new. You want to send me away to school. You want to make a Pale Face out of me." Joseph paused to study the effect of his words, but Sir William was toying idly with a quill. "I am a Mohawk." he continued. "My people want me at Canajoharie."

Sir William stabbed the desk with his quill. "So that's it," he whispered. Aloud he said, "I can understand your feelings, Joseph. I know the Mohawks, too. I don't want you to be a Pale Face, my boy. I want you to be a Mohawk, the greatest of all the Mohawks. I saw possibilities in you when you were a little lad. You've worked hard. You've never given me any reason to doubt you. In fact, I'm proud of you, Joseph."

"I am thankful," Joseph replied. "If you not bring me here, I not read. I not talk English. But I am Indian, Warraghiyagey. I can be nothing in your world. I am ambitious. I would be a leader." He stopped, surprised that he had told his hopes to any man.

"You'll be a leader, Joseph. Sometimes I think God has willed it. There is something about you which demands respect. That is why I want you to go to Connecticut to school."

"But why?"

"Sorry times are ahead, my boy, sorry times for the Indian. When I came to this country twenty years ago, there were few white settlers. The Mohawks hunted and fished as they wished. Now their lands have been taken away, piece by piece, by selfish white men. I am a Pale Face, Joseph. I know the weaknesses of my race. Hendrick also knew. He often said that the Mohawks could not beat the Pale Face by fighting against him. You remember, Joseph?"

In the Mohawk's mind flashed the scene at Fort Johnson eight years before. He saw his old friend sitting before a dying fire. He recalled Hendrick's warning and his prophecy.

"I remember well," he admitted.

"The Mohawk must be able to understand the Pale Face. He must talk the white man's language. He must be able to read and to write. He must meet the Pale Face in council, to deliberate, to fight back with words for things he can't get by the tomahawk.

"Hendrick noticed that you were the most promising lad in his nation. He hoped to live until you had become a man. Alas, my dear friend will never see the fine man you've turned out to be, Joseph. But he would be pleased. And he would be happy if you would finish your education so that you would be better able than he was to deal with the problems which face the Mohawks."

"But—the hunt? And the warpath?"

"Do you worry about your ability to carry on these things?"

The young Mohawk held his tongue.

"You've inherited those things, Joseph. I have seen you in battle. You never need worry about that part of your job. But there is much for you to learn in order to deal with the Pale Face. That is why I want you to go to Dr. Wheelock's school. Mr. Fowler will be away three days talking to the Oneidas. If you decide to go back with him, be ready by Wednesday. That is all, Joseph. I have told you my reasons why I want you to go. It is for *you* to make the decision."

On Wednesday at dawn Joseph left Fort Johnson with David Fowler. Two other Mohawk lads accompanied them; Neyges, a handsome, careless fellow, and Center, who coughed frequently as the party rode down the Mohawk Valley.

Chapter X

"I Would Try."

THE Mohawk lads arrived in Lebanon on the first day of August. They were hot, hungry, tired. Center coughed continually after they struck the low lands of the Connecticut River. Neyges wanted to turn back. Joseph learned the reason for the unhappiness of Neyges; the Mohawk loved a maiden of the Lower Castle and he would not be satisfied until he returned to her.

The first sight of the Moor Charity School disgusted Neyges. In the field near the house a group of Indians, stripped to the waist, were hoeing corn. A middle-aged white man, his shirt sleeves rolled to the elbows, was working harder than any of the boys.

"Ugh," grunted Neyges, "women."

Joseph did not reply. David Fowler had told him about Wheelock's educational ideas. Nothing had been said to Neyges or Center.

"I'm going home," announced Neyges, turning his horse.

Joseph grasped the bridle. "Not yet, Neyges," he said. "Let us try it for a moon."

"Not for a day," argued the stubborn Neyges.

Center coughed, but said nothing.

David Fowler listened anxiously. He had gone through the same experience. It had taken Wheelock months to convince him. To speak to these Mohawks now would be useless. He waved a hand to the man in shirt-sleeves.

Eleazer Wheelock dropped his hoe and came toward them. The preacher wore no wig. His graying hair was

50

thinning at the temples. Beads of perspiration stood out on his broad forehead.

"Welcome home, David," he said to Fowler, who dismounted to shake hands. "Did you have a good trip?"

"A splended one, Sir. I shall tell you all about it tonight. First I would like to have you meet these Mohawk lads."

Joseph slid from his horse, followed by Neyges and Center. Wheelock's eyes narrowed as they surveyed the smallest Mohawk. Center was ragged; he was dirty; he was ill. Quick consumption, probably; that disease was common among the Indians. It would have been better if David had left this boy with his parents.

Neyges was looking beyond Dr. Wheelock at the Indians in the cornfield. Scorn lowered the corners of his proud lips and emphasized the tilt of his head. Neyges was little better than naked. A torn shirt hung from one shoulder. His breechclout was filthy. The average Pale Face would have frowned at the sight of him, might have wrinkled his nose to keep out the body smell.

Wheelock did neither. He merely studied Neyges, seeing in him the primitive savage, dirty, yes, but proud, defiant, unconquerable. Neyges would not last at Lebanon. He would not bow to the routine which Wheelock had established. But it would interesting to have a try at him.

Fowler introduced the Mohawks. Center coughed. Neyges grunted. Joseph put out his hand and said carefully, "We are glad to meet you, Mr. Wheelock."

What Wheelock saw pleased him. This young man was not like the others. Joseph was dirty, to be sure, after the long journey, but it was not the permanent coating which covered his companions. His hunting shirt was not torn; it fitted his shoulders; open at the front, it exposed a brown chest. He wore leggings, tight to his legs, fringed, beaded. His moccasins were soft and well-fitting.

Wheelock's quick glance took in these features. It left them to study the young Mohawk's face. There were

handsomer Indians than Joseph Thayendanegea. Some
members of his own tribe were taller, heavier, more
powerful. Joseph stood erect, his shoulders balanced
easily, his hips narrow. He was not smiling. He seldom
smiled. But there was something in his face which
pleased Eleazer Wheelock. The preacher suspected there
might be a few drops of white blood in the young man's
veins, but the high cheekbones and the proud lips told of
generations of Indian ancestry. The keen eyes were also
those of an Indian.

"I am pleased to meet *you*, Joseph," said Wheelock.
"He is the lad Sir William has written me about?" he
asked Fowler.

"Yes. Joseph has lived at Fort Johnson for eight years,
since he was a boy of eleven. Sir William is proud of
Joseph, who has learned to speak English well. He can
also read some and has tried to write."

"And you wish to learn more?" Wheelock asked the
Mohawk.

"I would try," was Joseph's response. He had come to
Lebanon to do his best. But he did not wish to hoe corn
like a woman.

Wheelock had been studying the Indians. Some of that
dirt would have to be removed before his wife would let
them into the house. To David he suggested, "You are
hot and tired after your long journey. Why don't you
take our brothers down to the brook for a swim? Mrs.
Wheelock will give you some soap. I must go back to my
work, for we have much to do before supper. I'll see you
at that time."

The swim refreshed the travellers. Wheelock's wife
found clothes for Neyges and Center. They looked quite
decent in the castoff Yankee garments, though Joseph
sensed, from the expression on Neyges' face, that the
proud fellow was unhappy. At the supper table they met
the dozen Indians who were to be their schoolmates.
Except for three Delawares, these boys were New England Indians. Neyges ignored them. Joseph acknowledged
the introductions coolly. Center merely coughed.

There were also four young white men at the table. Charles Jeffrey Smith, recently ordained as a minister, acted as Wheelock's assistant. Samuel Kirkland, from nearby Norwich, was studying to be a missionary among the Indians. Wheelock's sons, John and James, completed the group.

Two weeks after Joseph's arrival in Lebanon, Samuel Kirkland came to him. The young man from Norwich was much liked by all residents at the school. The day's work was over and Joseph was walking toward the woods which fringed the Wheelock farm. He wanted to get away by himself for a few moments to avoid Center's coughing and the continued complaining of Neyges. Hearing steps behind him, he turned around.

Samuel Kirkland walked with free, easy strides. His slim body was erect and active. "Good evening, Joseph," he said. His smile was open, sincere, friendly. "I saw you start out. I thought you might like company."

Joseph did not want a companion. He wished to be alone. But Kirkland's smile disarmed him. "I'd like your company, Mr. Kirkland," he admitted, "but I must go back soon. Mr. Wheelock has rules."

Kirkland nodded. The rules were for Indians, not for him. "I have something to ask you, Joseph. Couldn't we sit here and talk for a few minutes?" He waved a hand at a snake fence that staggered along the edge of the pasture.

"If you wish, Mr. Kirkland."

Once they sat side by side with their feet braced against the lower rail, Kirkland broke into a laugh. "Mr. Wheelock is so formal about everything," he remarked. "How old are you, Joseph?"

"Nineteen."

"I'll be twenty on the first day of December. You need not address me as Mr. Kirkland. It makes me feel as if I were wearing a white beard. My name is Sam."

Joseph made no comment, but Kirkland's informality pleased him.

"You'll call me by my first name, Joseph?"

"Yes, Sam."

"Good. I'll tell you what I want. You know why I am here?"

"David Fowler told me."

"My father is a minister in Norwich. I hope to follow the same calling, but there will be a difference. Father works with white people. I wish to give my service to the Indians."

"It is a fine thing you want to do."

"I need help, Joseph. I must learn the Iroquois dialects if I am to communicate with your people. I have spoken to Mr. Wheelock, and he has consented to release you from farm work if you will help me to master the Mohawk language."

Joseph let his eyes rove across the fields. The corn, tall and green, waved its tassels in the wind. Joseph thought it much better than the Indian product. He could go back and teach his people to raise better crops. But his heart was not in farming. He had come to Lebanon to be educated in books. Mr. Wheelock had complimented him on the progress he was making. Now the preacher had confidence enough in him to recommend him as a tutor for this bright young man from Norwich. It would be an opportunity to exchange thoughts which pour from quick minds, thoughts which he had wasted on Neyges and Center. It would also mean loss of the hunting season, that event so dear to the heart of the Mohawk.

Joseph struggled with himself. He saw not the waving cornfields, but the straggling settlement at Canajoharie with its dirt, laziness and neglect. He saw also King Hendrick and remembered his teachings; he recalled what Sir William had said to him before he left Fort Johnson.

"I shall be glad to help you as much as I can," he promised Kirkland, "but when I talk my thoughts in English it is like passing a flower over the fire to you. What I think wilts, and the flower has lost its perfume."

"I shall be grateful for the wilted flower," said the young man from Norwich. "We'll start tomorrow, for I have much to learn."

When Joseph did not report at the field on the following day, Neyges broke out in open revolt. Who was Joseph Thayendanegea that he should sit in a classroom with a Pale Face while another future brave took care of horses?

Affairs came to a head in October. Joseph, sitting before a table with Sam Kirkland, heard angry words rise from the yard. He rushed to the window.

The two sons of Eleazer Wheelock were standing side by side, their faces crimson and their fists clenched at their sides. Before them crouched Neyges, who clutched a knife in his right hand.

"For the last time I'll ask you, will you saddle my horse?" John Wheelock's voice rose to a shout.

Neyges shook his head. He did not retreat a step.

"Don't you know, you stupid Indian, that I am a gentleman's son?" Young Wheelock thundered.

There was no reply from Neyges.

James Wheelock spoke up. "Do you know what a gentleman is?" he asked the Mohawk.

"I do," said Neyges, straightening up. "He is man who keep race horse. He drink wine. That your father not do. He no gentleman. Go saddle horse yourself." With head erect and shoulders squared, he walked into the barn.

It was the final straw. For some time Eleazer Wheelock had been planning to send Center home. It was clear that Neyges should go, too, for he would not obey orders. Wheelock called in Joseph. He told the lad that Center and Neyges must go home on the morrow.

"You may go or stay as you wish, Joseph," said Wheelock. "I would like to have you stay, for you are being of help to Mr. Kirkland. If you decide to go home with Neyges and Center, I would like to leave something with you for you to think about." Wheelock paused, as if making ready to choose the exact words he wished to use.

"The first thing God set man about," he told Joseph, "and that before he ever had sinned, when he was more honorable than any man has been ever since, was to till the ground to get his living by it. The earth is all God's land, and he will have it all cultivated. So long as there are not enough people to inhabit the earth, God lets the wild beasts have it for their dwelling place; and a few lazy, savage people he suffers to live a hungry, miserable life by hunting.

"But when the children of men grow numerous and want the earth to cultivate for the living, the wild beasts must give place to them and men must improve the land for God. If they do not, they are bad tenants and must be turned off as such. If you will not cultivate God's land, you cannot expect that God will greatly multiply you."

Joseph listened carefully. It was not often that Wheelock talked to him in this way. He flushed to the roots of his hair at Wheelock's reference to the Indian as a lazy savage. "The Indian is not lazy," he answered, surprised at his own boldness. "The Indian is a hunter. He can shoot game. He can live and not work in the field like a woman."

"And when the game is gone?" Wheelock asked.

"He can move on to more land."

"If you Indians would improve your land and provide a living for yourselves and families in that way, you would live much easier and better than you now do or ever can do by hunting. And when the game is gone, you will not have to move to another place or to go a great way to catch wild creatures to live upon, as Indians have been forced to do; but you will live as well without them as with them, by the produce of your own farms.

"I have thus spoken to you, Joseph, because I think you have common sense enough to see my position. You have lived long with white men. You know that their numbers are increasing, while the Indians are on the decline. Before not too many years, the whites will greatly outnumber your people in the Mohawk Valley. You must learn to live with them, to cultivate the fields as they do."

It could have been Sir William talking, or King Hendrick. Joseph had no argument. So he said, "I will stay here a little longer and help Mr. Kirkland. Neyges can take Center home."

Joseph got home for the hunting season. With him went Sam Kirkland, to meet Sir William and to study conditions among the Mohawks and the Oneidas. They stayed at Fort Johnson during the month of November. Kirkland spent much time with the Oneidas. Neyges married. Center died. Shortly after the snow goose had dumped its first handful of feathers over the valley, Wheelock's two students returned to Lebanon, bringing with them three young Mohawk lads.

A year passed. Kirkland entered Princeton College. Mr. Smith, Wheelock's assistant, was preparing to take a trip to the Iroquois country. He wrote Sir William for permission to take Joseph with him as interpreter. Johnson consented. Joseph was willing. Smith went to New York to make final arrangements for the trip.

Meanwhile Pontiac was stirring the western Indians to revolt against the white settlers in the Ohio River Valley. Molly, watching developments from Fort Johnson, kept Joseph informed of each move Pontiac made.

The Mohawk lad appeared before Eleazer Wheelock one morning. He held a letter from Molly in his hand. The Mohawks, displeased because he stayed at school when war was brewing, demanded that he return at once.

Eleazer Wheelock did not argue. He gave him one of his best horses and told him to go home. "The time of parting has come, Joseph," he said. "You have endeared yourself to me, to Mr. Smith, and to everybody else here. We shall not forget you. In my prayers I have often mentioned three things I wish you and your people to do. It is to live as good subjects, to fear God and to honor the King. You will remember?"

"I'll not forget," Joseph promised.

Wheelock smiled as he shook hands. He did not suspect that his words would be thrown back at him a decade later.

Chapter XI

"I Shall Lead More Than My Own Nation."

THE campaign against Pontiac proved a wonderful experience for Joseph. He saw much new country. He met the Western Indians and sensed immediately that they were not like the Mohawks. Their relations had been with the French, who were hostile toward the British. They were hunters and trappers and warriors. They cared not a fig for white civilization.

He studied Pontiac carefully at the great council at Lake Ontario. The Ottawa chief spoke fluently, but Joseph saw little to admire in this man who had become the leader of his people. Pontiac did not have the interests of the Indians at heart. He did not wish to lead them. He wanted to master them. Pontiac talked much of cooperation at Lake Ontario but Joseph did not believe him. If the Indians were to be united, it would not be under the Ottawa chief.

A true leader of the Indians would be something like Sir William Johnson. He would not force his ideas upon them. He would suggest new things and encourage the people to try them out before accepting them. And if the ideas were turned down, he would not insist upon having his own way.

Sir William was making an experiment of this kind now. He had built a new home in the wilderness above Fort Johnson, a frame mansion flanked by two stone blockhouses. The Irishman called this new house Johnson Hall. To it he planned to bring all that was best in agriculture, landscaping, literature and art. The fields would be cultivated by modern methods. There would be flower gardens and shade trees. Sir William was already purchasing books for his library and paintings for his drawing room.

A village was springing up around the mansion. Settlers were coming in daily, not because they had to come, but because they saw in Sir William's experiment something that would mean much to their future lives. Johnstown was not to be an ordinary settlement, with a few log houses between muddy roads and the forest. Its new schoolhouse was already in operation and a courthouse was being raised. And Gilbert Tice's tavern was doing a rushing business. Yes, Johnstown was the ideal place in which to settle.

Joseph went up to the new settlement to visit his sister. He was amazed at the size of the house, but a frown crossed his face at sight of the stone blockhouses. What did they mean in a time of peace? There was no danger from the Western Indians. The Iroquois were friendly. Why had Sir William fortified his new home? Could he see farther ahead than other people? Was he expecting war?

Of late there had been much talk about a Stamp Act that had been passed by Parliament in that mother country far across the Great Lake. Sir William had been worried when people in a town called Boston had refused to accept the stamps. But that was all over now. The stamps had been taken back. An era of peace had settled over the Mohawk Valley. Except for disagreements over land, the Indian and the Pale Face were living side by side in the settlements along the river. And yet Sir William had built blockhouses. Joseph did not understand it.

Molly told him of changes that had come about since his departure. Johnny Johnson, having completed his schooling at Philadelphia, was in England adding to his education. Sir William's two daughters had married. Polly was the wife of Guy Johnson. They were living at Guy

Park, a new stone mansion on the Mohawk River. Daniel
Claus, the German interpreter, had won Nancy's hand.

"I shall marry, too," said Joseph.

"Have you anyone in mind?"

Joseph had a girl in mind. He had met her at Oneida
Castle when he had gone there with Sam Kirkland. He
could see her now. She was slender as a birch sapling.
Her hair was black as night. And when she smiled, all the
warmth of spring shone from her eyes.

"Yes," Joseph replied, "I shall marry Christina, the
Oneida maiden."

"You should marry a Mohawk," Molly chided him.

Joseph winked an eye. "Did you?" he asked.

Molly stamped her foot. "I am a woman," she said. "I
don't count. You are a man and a warrior. You may
soon be a chief. You will want to lead your people."

"I shall lead more than my own nation." Joseph stood
before her, tall, lean, capable. He was no longer the little
brother.

"You have dreams, Joseph," Molly said, "but don't let
them carry you away. The Mohawks may not want you
to marry an Oneida."

"They can like it or not," he retorted hotly. "I shall
go to Mother tomorrow."

His mother was won over by his arguments. A canoe
travelled swiftly up the Mohawk River, bearing the
mother and son. At Fort Stanwix the pair left the river
and took the trail to Oneida Castle. Joseph waited while
a proposition of marriage was made to the mother of
Christina.

The following afternoon three people rode in the
canoe as it approached the Upper Castle at Canajoharie.
The proud fellow in the stern was Joseph Brant, dressed
in a green coat Sir William had given him. His mother
reclined in the waist of the canoe. He had no eyes for
her. All he could see was the slender form of Christina,
who plied her paddle from the bow. Her hair reached to
her waist; into its blackness she had woven strands of

colored ribbon. The beads on her dress sparkled as her shoulders moved with each stroke of the paddle. She would turn around occasionally to smile at Joseph, and that young brave would feel the blood surge into his cheeks at the sight of the brown face with its shy eyes and inviting lips.

The canoe grated on the shore. The mother stepped out. Joseph held a hand to Christina, who took it shyly. Together, they followed the mother to the Brant house. The girl carried some cakes of Indian corn wrapped in bark. She handed them to Joseph's mother as a symbol of her ability to do the housework. The older woman gave her in return some venison to be sent to her mother. This gift was to prove that Joseph was able to support her daughter. The wedding ceremony was over. Christina was Joseph's wife.

Chapter XII

"I Have Looked into Your Heart."

J OSEPH built a bark house for Christina at Canajoharie. Two children blessed their union, a boy whom they called Isaac and a girl who bore her mother's name. The Brant home became a stopping place for Indians and for Pale Faces. Councils took place there. White missionaries spent the night with Joseph on their way to visit the Oneidas and the Onondagas. Samuel Kirkland, who had failed to convert the Senecas and was now instructing the Oneidas, became a frequent visitor. So did Nicholas Herkimer, a prosperous German farmer who had built a new house near the Little Falls.

Joseph went often to Johnson Hall, where he worked with Guy Johnson, who was being trained to step into Sir William's shoes. Here he also met John Butler and his son Walter, a surly young man who was preparing to study law in Albany. He distrusted the Butlers at first sight. But he liked Daniel Claus. The interpreter seemed to understand him and sympathized with his plans for the future.

Joseph learned that Sir William did not like the way people were acting in the seaboard cities. That new Governor, William Tryon, was having a peck of trouble trying to straighten things out in New York. Claus considered Tryon a blunderer who would lead the colony into war.

They also talked of Sir William's health. The Irishman had never recovered from the wound he had received at Lake George. Lately he had been troubled with pains in his hip. He also suffered from dysentery. Only a short time before he had gone with the Mohawks to a place called Saraghtoga. The medicinal waters had failed to help him.

Joseph talked to Claus about Christina. Since the birth of their second child, Joseph's wife had been ailing. A stubborn cough kept her awake nights. Indian remedies did her no good.

"Why don't you have Sir William's doctor see her?" asked Daniel.

Joseph frowned. "Christina doesn't trust white doctors. She still believes in Indian medicine. Maybe she will come along all right."

He didn't believe his own statement and Claus knew it. Daniel insisted that he take the doctor down to Canajoharie to see Christina.

The doctor's examination confirmed Claus' worst fears. Christina had consumption. She could live but a short time.

Joseph accepted the truth with a heavy heart. To most Indians, a wife was a mere slave, one to bear him children and to do the heavy work while he hunted or fished. He had been brought up among white men. To him, Christina was a companion who could share his joys and sorrows.

So when Christina died and was laid to rest in the Indian graveyard at Canajoharie, he wanted to throw himself in the river.

Sir William sent for him. "You must brace up, my boy," he said. "You can't mope around. You'll only make yourself sick. You've got to find work. It's the only way to save yourself."

Joseph listened respectfully. He had nothing to say.

"I have a proposition to make you," said Sir William. "There is at Fort Hunter near the Lower Castle a minister of the church. His name is John Stuart. He is trying to educate the Mohawks in the Christian religion. He wants a Mohawk to act as interpreter and to help him translate some hymns into your language. I'm recommending you to him, Joseph. You are the only man around here who can help him. And by helping Mr. Stuart you will be helping yourself."

Joseph left his children with his mother at Canajoharie and paddled down the river. Mr. Stuart, six feet four in his stockinged feet, greeted him with friendliness.

Joseph went to work. One of the first hymns he tried to translate was the "Veni Creator." He read the first verse carefully in English:

> "Come, Holy Ghost, Creator, Come:
> Inspire the souls of Thine
> Till ev'ry heart which Thou has made
> Is filled with Grace divine."

The Mohawk alphabet consisted of only sixteen letters, with no labial sounds such as b, f, l, m, p, or v. The Mohawks never could understand why a Pale Face closed his mouth in order to talk. So it was some time before Joseph had the first verse ready.

Filled with pride, he took it to Mr. Stuart. The minister did his pupil the honor of reading it aloud in his uncertain Mohawk:

> "Ka ro Ro ni gough yough stouh
> Ne Sa kiven yat ni yoh,
> O ni a give gouh tak we yegho
> Sa wea na do geagh ty."

Other hymn translations followed. Soon a book of songs was ready for use in Stuart's Indian chapel at Fort Hunter.

Joseph took to religion hard. He joined the Episcopal Church. He also was admitted to the Masonic fraternity. He even tried his hand at a translation of the Book of Mark.

While he was at Fort Hunter, he made one of those friendships which were peculiar to the Mohawks. It was a custom of Joseph's people for a warrior to select a friend to whom he could tell his secrets. They could also share each other's joys and sorrows. Joseph attached himself to Captain John Provost, a young British officer at the fort.

The officer liked Joseph. He returned the friendship, but he did not suspect how seriously the Mohawk regarded it. They hunted together. They shared each other's food. They talked over their most intimate problems.

One day in summer they were sitting on a log after catching a string of trout for Mr. Stuart's table.

"John," said Joseph, "ever since the willows sent their baby leaves to greet the sun, a little bird has been whispering in my ear."

Provost said nothing. Once Joseph got into this mood, interruptions were useless.

"And what has the little bird been whispering? You want to know, John?"

Provost was too bewildered to answer.

"The little bird has been whispering for me to look into your heart, John."

The Captain raised his eyes.

"I have looked into your heart," cried Joseph, his face shining. "And I have discovered there my true blood brother. You are my brother, John?"

"Why—why of course." Provost acted surprised.

Joseph drew his hunting knife from its sheath. "And we shall always be blood brothers?" he asked.

"Always." Provost still did not understand.

Joseph bared his forearm. Carefully, with the tip of the blade, he cut the brown skin. Blood trickled down his arm.

He handed the knife to Provost and said, "You do it, too."

Provost rolled up his sleeve. Without realizing the meaning of his act, he broke the skin of his forearm and stared at his own blood.

Joseph seized Provost's arm and pressed it against his own. The blood from the two wounds mingled as it rolled down their fingers.

The Mohawk chanted some words in his native tongue which Provost did not understand. Then Joseph cried, "Your blood has mingled with mine and mine with

yours, John. My heart beats fast with yours, my Brother.
You are no longer John Provost. I am no longer Joseph
Brant. We are one and the same person. We are true
blood brothers and my heart is glad."

They staunched the flow of blood and washed their
arms in the brook which ran at their feet. Joseph took
out his pipe and filled it with tobacco. He asked Provost
to do likewise. The Mohawk handed his pipe to the
Captain and received that of Provost in return. They
smoked each other's pipes before returning to Fort
Hunter.

Such friendship was not enough for Joseph. He could
not live without a wife. Christina's sister had attracted
him. He decided to marry her. He asked Mr. Stuart to
perform a Christian ceremony.

Stuart refused. "It is against the rules of the Church
of England for a man to marry his wife's sister," he told
Joseph.

"But I love Susanna and she loves me," the Mohawk
argued.

"I'm sorry. I cannot and I will not do it."

Joseph's anger flared. "Very well," he retorted, "I'll
have the Dutch dominie marry us."

The Dutch preacher performed the ceremony. Joseph
left Fort Hunter with Susanna for the Upper Castle at
Canajoharie, for the Mohawks were looking to him for
protection against the land hunger of the Pale Face.
Joseph, with his English education, could see how his
people had been cheated. He was particularly angry with
one George Klock, a Dutchman who surveyed the Canajoharie tract by moonlight and secured a patent without
the consent of the Mohawks. Klock, when cornered,
refused to sign a release.

Governor William Tryon of New York came to Johnson Hall to visit Sir William and to listen to the grievances of the Mohawks. The sachems of Canajoharie met
in council before leaving the village and agreed that they
had labored in vain. It would be better to put their

business into the hands of the young warriors. They chose Joseph Brant to speak for them.

A great circle had formed on the grass before Johnson Hall when Joseph rose to speak. It was a proud moment for the young Mohawk, for his first appearance as a speaker was to be made before the governor of the colony. It was a nervous moment, too, for Tryon's surly face offered him little encouragement. The governor was not pleased at the news that the sachems had put their business into the hands of the warriors. Such a step often meant war.

Joseph was aware that the words of an orator should flow from the tongue of a panther who had lapped from a pot of oil. "Brothers," he began, "we are extremely happy to see you here this day. We have long desired it and we hope that through your means we shall obtain justice. We have been often deceived and cheated out of large tracts of land; but that which gives us most concern is the little tract on which we live and which is likely to be taken from us. This fills us with much concern. It is also of so alarming a nature that whether we are in our beds or roaming the woods in search of game, it still occurs to us and we cannot sleep.

"Brothers, we hope to obtain redress through your love of justice and from the great character which we received of you both before and since your arrival. We therefore have the strongest hopes of meeting with that justice from you which hitherto we have applied for in vain."

He went on to tell of the loyalty of the Mohawks to the British in war. He reminded Tryon that the white officers and soldiers had been rewarded for their services with tracts of land, whereas the Mohawks were being robbed of their homes. He spoke bitterly of George Klock. This fellow had surveyed the Canajoharie tract by moonlight. Such a survey was illegal. Klock has refused to sign a release even though he had been hauled up before Governor Moore four years before. Something must be done about Klock, and very soon.

"We are at present but a small number," he concluded, "but our connections are powerful and our alliances many. Should any of these see that the faithful Mohawks are ill used and cheated, it may alarm them and lead to dangerous consequences."

Governor Tryon flushed at this threat of war. He answered Joseph the next day. He was glad to hear of the grievances at first hand. He would order a survey at which the Mohawks would be represented. He praised the Indians for their bravery on the warpath and for their faithfulness to the King. But he did not like the idea of the sachems giving way to the young warriors.

"In a state of war," said Tryon, "I would deal with warriors, but in a time of peace, I ask you to restore the power to the sachems. I shall interpret your refusal as a want of confidence on your part in the public justice of this government. You have King George for your protector, and under him his representative. Therefore you do not need warriors to support your present cause, especially while you are in the possession of the lands in question."

The sachems gave in to Tryon.

Joseph saw through the Governor. Tryon talked of peace at a time when the country was seething with revolt. The old liar; he was trying to pull the wool over the eyes of the Indians. Tryon knew nothing of George Klock, who would cheat a Mohawk out of his eye teeth. The situation could not be handled by scolding the sachems and patting the backs of the warriors. He resolved to fight to a finish.

Chapter XIII

"Take Care of My People."

WHEN Joseph paddled down to Fort Hunter to talk with the Mohawks of the Lower Castle, he found the British regiment preparing to leave.

The Mohawk saw John Provost in his room. The captain had finished packing.

"What is the meaning of this?" asked Joseph, his face showing his anxiety.

"We've been ordered to the West Indies," Provost's smile was forced.

"But why?"

"The fortunes of war, Joseph. There have been exciting times in Boston. The people dressed up as Indians and dumped the King's tea into the harbor rather than pay a tax on it. New York and Charleston also refused to take our tea. Our regiment has been called away to protect our trade in the West Indies. It looks like war, my friend."

Joseph accepted the facts without understanding them. He had been out of touch with recent affairs in Boston and New York. The truth dawned upon him; John Provost, his blood brother, was leaving, possibly forever. To the Indian's mind, this was a serious matter. He could no longer live if Provost went away.

"You cannot go, John," he said.

"And why not?" asked Provost. "I belong to a regiment. Where the regiment goes, I go."

"But you are also attached to me," Joseph protested.

Provost was Joseph's blood brother, but he had never

understood what such a friendship might mean to an Indian. He saw how difficult it would be to say goodbye. "Yes," he admitted, "I am attached to you, Joseph. I love you as a brother. We have had many good times together. But, when duty calls, a soldier must go where he is sent, regardless of relatives or friends. It is one of the sad things about war."

"You cannot go!" cried Joseph. "You cannot take a chance on your life. I shall go in your place."

Provost steeled himself for a reply. "It's no use, Joseph," he told the Mohawk. "I appreciate everything you have done for me. I admire you more than any man I have ever known. But I, too, am a warrior. You would be ashamed to know me if I stayed at home when duty called."

"But I cannot live without you," Joseph argued. "I am part of you. You are part of me. I shall be only half a man if you go away."

Provost smiled. "Never fear," he said. "There is no danger of your losing your manhood." A bugle sounded outside the fort. He picked up his knapsack and slung it over his shoulder. "Goodbye, my dear brother," he said, embracing Joseph. "It may be that we shall meet again some day."

Joseph stood in the doorway, stunned, bewildered. The regiment was parading before the fort. Batteaux awaited them in the river. He rushed off to see Mr. Stuart.

The minister listened to Joseph's story. He knew the relationship between the Mohawk and Provost. He was also aware that the officer had not felt it so keenly as had the Indian. No white man could.

"Don't be so sorrowful, Joseph," said Stuart. "Console yourself with another friend. Myself, for instance."

"No," cried Joseph, "I cannot do that. I am John's brother and I cannot have another brother at the same time. I shall go home now. I shall send John a present. I shall send him the finest suit of furs the world has ever seen. When he wears it, he will again be part of me and I of him."

Stuart was tempted to smile at Joseph's knowledge of geography. Of what use would a coat of furs be in the West Indies? But Stuart said, "That will be splendid, Joseph. I know John will be very happy to receive the gift."

Joseph's cup of sorrow was to be filled to overflowing the following summer. Sir William Johnson's old wound had never healed. The trip to the springs at Saraghtoga had offered no relief. Yet he carried on at a time when the earth trembled beneath his feet.

Joseph visited Johnson Hall in July. Indians had come from all directions. They trampled Sir William's flowers. They pulled vegetables out of his gardens. They stole everything on which they could lay their hands. The day of the council broke hot and sultry. Sir William spoke to them at length.

Joseph watched him with troubled eyes. Sir William's face grew red and puffy. The lilting voice did not have its usual ring. The Irishman was unsteady on his feet. It seemed to Joseph that he would be unable to finish his speech, but he struggled to the end and closed with a fiery challenge to the Indians for support.

"I am tired," he said to Joseph, who had helped him to his room. "Maybe you'd better send for Johnny." He dropped on the bed.

Joseph stared at him, for Sir William's breath was coming hard. The Mohawk called a servant. "Send a horseman to Fort Johnson. John is to come right away. Do not spare the horses." The servant turned. "Wait," said Joseph, taking matters into his own hands, "have the doctor sent up right away."

Sir William tried to smile. "I heard you, Joseph," he gasped. "A doctor's of no use now, my boy. My work is done." He cried out with pain and fell back on the bed.

"What is it?" Joseph became thoroughly alarmed.

"My heart's give out," whispered his old friend. His

voice could hardly be heard. "One thing I must say to you, Joseph. We are in for difficult times. The Pale Faces are at each other's throats. There will be a war, Joseph."

The Mohawk nodded agreement.

"It will go hard with the Indians, my boy. I have tried my best to help them. Guy is a fine man. He will do his best, but his best may not be enough." Sir William's voice became so faint that Joseph had to bend over him to hear it. "Joseph, you are the true leader of your people. Fight for your rights. Take care of your people, Joseph, take—care—"

The tree had fallen!

Joseph turned to the window. Outside, on the broad expanse of green, the Indians were making merry. A keg of rum had been rolled inside the circle, then a second keg and a third. The warriors were attacking them with the ferocity of redskins on the warpath.

"Take care of my people," Joseph muttered. "Take—care—of—my—people."

Chapter XIV

"That Is My Answer."

NEWS of Sir William's death flew like wildfire through the Mohawk Valley. Delegations of Indians and whites appeared at the funeral. There was much sincere mourning, but some individuals rejoiced that the Irishman had passed away. These men, who called themselves Whigs, began to show their true colors. Committees opposed to the King sprang up in the settlements along the river. The winter was filled with tense sparring between Guy Johnson and these Whig committees.

Late in April a horseman rode up the Valley. He carried news of the fighting between British regulars and Minutemen at Lexington and Concord in Massachusetts. The Whigs called a meeting at Canaughwaga on the Mohawk River, where they planned to erect a liberty pole. Guy Johnson did not like the looks of things. He decided to ride to the meeting. Joseph Brant and a band of armed retainers went with him.

They found Canaughwaga seething with excitement. Hundreds of farmers had come to the meeting; they had brought with them their wives and families. It was a beautiful day in May. The affair took on the air of a picnic, for most of the people hadn't the slightest idea why they had come. The wives and children laughed and played, while the men gathered in knots, some to explain, others to argue.

Many Tories attended. Joseph could see John Johnson astride his horse, his face redder than usual. The Butlers rode at John's side. They stared sullenly at the farmers.

Daniel Claus waved to Joseph, who returned the friendly greeting.

Colonel Guy Johnson watched the farmers gather around the liberty pole. The colonel, a serious, conscientious officer, had tried hard to keep the reins tight in his hands. He had fought off charges made against his handling of Indian affairs. He had threatened to punish writers of unsigned letters abusing him. It had all been of no use. What could an Irish gentleman do against this rabble?

A man was addressing the farmers. His arms swung around like windmills. His thick Dutch voice grated upon Guy's ears. "Down with the King!" the man shouted. "Down with all the Johnsons!"

Guy touched a spur to his horse. The animal burst through the crowd, brushing aside shrieking men and women. The colonel's face was purple. His hand grasped the hilt of his sword.

The orator saw Guy coming. He was a man of words but not of action. He fled before the officer in the green coat.

Guy had never been madder in his life, though he was known as a man of temper. Facing the crowd, he yelled, "Listen to me, you fools! Who are you to curse the King and to criticize his chosen officers? Who are you to utter careless words about the Johnson family?"

His trumpetlike voice brought quiet to his audience. "You talk of taking up arms against the King," he said scornfully. "Do you know the strength of that King? Do you realize that he can put down any insurrection you start like that?" Guy snapped his fingers. The sound carried to the whole audience, so tense was the silence. "You talk of fighting him on the sea. Fools! A single frigate could capture all the navy you could float. You have talked with the Indians. You have tried to undermine all Sir William has done to bring peace to this valley. I say you are ungrateful people. The Indians are more appreciative of favors granted. They are all for their Father the King, from the Gulf of St. Lawrence to the Mississippi River."

A young Whig farmer stepped from the crowd. He pressed close to the speaker's horse and lifted his chin toward Guy Johnson. His hands rested lightly on his hips. In an insolent voice he cried, "Guy Johnson, you are a liar and a villain!"

Johnson reached down and seized his tormenter by the shoulder. The armed Tories pressed through the crowd. The young farmer was knocked on the head with the butt of a riding whip. One of Guy's servants sat astride of him, pummelling his body. The farmer, a tough fellow, threw off the servant and rushed at Johnson. Two pistols were pressed to his chest. He halted, bewildered. He was knocked down again. Guy wheeled his horse and rode off, followed by John Johnson, the Butlers, Joseph Brant and the Tories. The unarmed crowd jeered them as they passed through.

The party rode silently down the river to Guy Park. Once inside his fortified home, Guy admitted his error. "I lost my head, Joseph," he said. "But what could a gentleman do, with that rabble insulting Sir William and the King?"

Joseph knew a better method. He and the Mohawks would have scalped and butchered the Whigs. Dead men tell no tales. But he kept his silence.

"We must make sure of the Indians," said Guy, once his anger had cooled. "What is the word from the Oneidas?"

"I sent them a message. It never got there. The Whigs must have intercepted it. Little can be done with the Oneidas. Sam Kirkland has them in the palm of his hand. I tried to get Kirkland removed, as you know, but you didn't think it should be done."

"We had nothing against him, Joseph. You can't convict a man who isn't guilty."

"He could have been made guilty."

Johnson ignored this comment. "We'll call a council here," he said.

Joseph merely grunted. Of what use were councils, now that the war had started? Rifles and powder and tomahawks and knives talked more effectively.

The council at Guy Park ended in failure. "We do not want to interfere in the dispute between old England and Boston," Little Abraham of the Lower Castle told Guy Johnson. "The white people may settle their own quarrels between themselves. We shall never meddle in those affairs, or be the aggressors, if we are let alone. We have for a long time lived in peace with one another and we wish ever to continue so."

With this speech Little Abraham gave up control of his nation. The warriors turned to Joseph Brant for leadership.

The Mohawk Valley was getting too hot for Guy Johnson. Toward the end of May he and his followers travelled up the Mohawk Valley, crossed Oneida Lake and stopped at Oswego. Here Guy won the allegiance of 1700 Indians. He rode on to Montreal, where he gained the good will of thousands more.

Joseph Brant went with Johnson. The Mohawk's mind was in conflict. He had been much impressed by Little Abraham's speech. After all, why shouldn't the white people settle their own disputes? The Indians had fought with the British against the French and vice versa. The Mohawks had lost many braves at Lake George, including the beloved Hendrick. What had they gained? Nothing, reasoned Joseph. The British victory had opened the way for that villain, George Klock, and other land speculators. In previous wars, the Six Nations had been a united people. Now Samuel Kirkland had pulled the Oneidas and the Tuscaroras away from the Confederacy.

Joseph was thinking of Sam Kirkland when a letter arrived from Reverend Eleazer Wheelock, who had always been a dissenter, in religion and in politics. He was now asking Joseph to use his influence in pulling the Indians to the side of the Bostonians. Joseph's mind flashed back to the parting with Wheelock and the words his teacher had spoken.

"Your letter recalled the many pleasures of my residence with you," he wrote Wheelock. "I remember particularly the prayers each evening, to which I lent both ears. There is one passage that cannot be erased from my memory. It was that we might all be able to live as good subjects, to fear God; and *to honor the King*. That is my answer."

He signed the letter, "Joseph Thayendanegea."

Chapter XV

"An Indian Chief Kisses No Man's Hand."

JOSEPH Brant visited England that winter as a member of a party which included Guy Johnson, Gilbert Tice, Daniel Claus, and John Deseronto, a Mohawk from the Lower Castle at Fort Hunter. They wanted to discover the attitude of the King and Parliament toward the uprising in America.

They stayed in London at The Swan with Two Necks, a famous tavern. The Indians, being curiosities in the British capital, were entertained by noted people. James Boswell, who wrote the biography of Samuel Johnson, was particularly kind to Joseph. It was he who asked the Mohawk to sit for a portrait by George Romney, one of the greatest painters of the time.

Joseph enjoyed himself in London. Like all Indians he loved pomp and ceremony, and the British court put on quite a show. But he never forgot that he had gone to England on business. He had an interview with George Germain, the Secretary for War, and explained fully why the Indians were not satisfied. Germain promised to do all he could to help them.

The two Mohawks were received at court by King George III. The reception room was crowded with men dressed in court uniforms and wearing all kinds of decorations. The ladies were powdered, perfumed and rouged. The fat King sat on a throne at one end of the room; beside him was the Queen.

Joseph watched the officers go before the King, bend their knees, and kiss the monarch's hand. The Mohawk wore a uniform, too. He might have been taken for a white man if he had not insisted upon wearing his Mohawk headdress with its three feathers. But anyone watching the scene would have noticed that he and John Deseronto were not like the other officers.

The two Mohawks stood apart, with their arms held rigidly to their sides. Their faces showed nothing. Yet this very lack of expression should have told the British that the Mohawks were not pleased at what they were seeing.

Guy Johnson watched them out of the corner of one eye. He may have read their thoughts, for his face looked worried. And when he brought them forward to present them to the King and Queen, he was prepared for almost anything.

Johnson bowed. So did Joseph and John Deseronto. Johnson knelt. The Indians stood erect.

Joseph, watching the King's face, did not know whether the monarch was displeased or amused. The Queen smiled.

The King extended a fat hand toward Johnson, who pressed his lips to the monarch's fingers.

Joseph watched this ceremony without twitching a muscle. His turn came next. Soon the King would stretch a hand to him with the lazy manner of a fat man.

The hand dangled before Joseph's eyes, white and puffy. The only nice thing about it was the ring, which sparkled.

What Johnson had feared came to pass. Joseph ignored the King's hand.

A murmur of voices sounded throughout the room. And Joseph knew that the courtiers were expressing their amazement at a man who refused to kiss the King's hand. Probably they were calling him a savage. They might even try to kill him.

A hand touched his sleeve. Guy Johnson was telling him to kiss the King's hand.

The Mohawk rose to his full height and stared the

King in the face. "An Indian chief kisses no man's hand," he said in a voice that all could hear.

King George let his hand drop to his knee. A flush crept over his cheeks. He had nothing to say in the face of this insult. The courtiers were too shocked to discuss such a breach of court etiquette.

The Queen put forth her hand. It was white; it was beautiful. On her lips lay the trace of a smile.

Joseph bowed low before her and said, "I have no objection to kissing the hand of a lady. Their hands are made to be kissed by men." He pressed his lips to the Queen's fingers. John Deseronto followed his example.

The Queen laughed and soon the King and the court saw humor in the situation. London would talk for years about the Mohawk who had refused to kiss the hand of a man but had not objected to kissing that of a woman.

It was at a fancy dress ball that Joseph Brant made his most striking impression on the British court. Joseph and John Deseronto had been persuaded by Daniel Claus to appear in native costume, so Joseph painted half of his face red and left the other side bare. He traced black circles around both eyes. His costume consisted of a green coat and fringed leggings. A tomahawk with "J. Thayendanegea" engraved upon it shone from his belt. A headdress of three feathers added a foot to his height.

Many kinds of costume graced the ball. Knights, hermits, gypsies and harlequins mingled together, all of them masked. A Turkish diplomat appeared in his native dress. He wandered around the great hall examining the costumes and talking with their wearers. He was a good-natured fellow who was enjoying himself.

He came up to Joseph Brant.

"Ah, what a splendid costume!" he exclaimed.

Joseph said nothing. His face looked like a mask.

The Turk's curiosity got the better of him. He pinched Joseph's nose.

This move caught Joseph by surprise. His hand went to his tomahawk. Rising to his toes, he cried out the scalp yell of the Mohawks, a clear piercing call that carried over every other sound in the room. Then, seizing the Turk by the collar, he stood over him and waved his tomahawk above the diplomat's head.

No one came to the Turk's rescue. He stood there, pale and trembling, thinking that each moment might be his last. The crowd was stampeded by this act of savagery. Gentle shepherdesses and fortune-telling crones shrieked and hurried away as fast as their ample skirts would permit. Knights in armor and hooded monks shrank from the sound of Joseph's voice. Those who had the courage to look back saw the Mohawk standing over the cowering Turk. His tomahawk flashed in circles around the head of his pretended victim.

Joseph, having enjoyed his fun, put the weapon back in his belt and strode with dignity across the room. The Turk saw that his experience had been merely a joke, while the masquers laughed nervously at their fears.

Chapter XVI

"My Trail Will Be Slippery with Blood."

JOSEPH and his friends sailed for America in the packet Harriet early in June. They sailed with confidence that the British government would give full support to the Loyalists and the Indians in their struggle against the Bostonians, for they carried with them promises from the King and from George Germain.

Rough seas slowed up the Harriet, which was driven off its course and overhauled near Bermuda by a privateer mounting several six-pound cannon. The Harriet, though undermanned and carrying only three-pounders, tried to fight back. The balls from the privateer's guns cut into her rigging. Her masts and sails were badly damaged. The privateer's captain brought his ship closer with the idea of boarding the packet. The Harriet's captain and crew resigned themselves to being taken as a prize of war.

Guy Johnson and the two Mohawks watched the fight from the rail, though the captain had ordered them to take cover. A frown creased Johnson's face.

"Gad, Joseph," he cried, "we can't stand here and be captured. We've got some important work to do. If these fellows take us, we'll get tossed into prison. We may have to cool our heels there until the war is over."

He rushed up to the captain, who stood near the bridge. "Captain," he cried, "we have simply got to fight off those fellows. You have on board this ship the leaders of our armies in the Colony of New York. You can't let us be taken."

The captain shrugged. "You've seen me do all I could to get away. We can't run any longer. And how can we keep those devils from boarding us?"

"I have some good marksmen with me. Two of them are Indians. Either of them can hit a squirrel between the eyes at fifty yards. Let us join your crew. We'll pick off a few of the leaders when the privateer draws closer. That will take the fight out of the crew."

The captain argued against this suggestion. "Why, they'll murder all of us in cold blood if you do that."

"It is better to die than to live in prison."

The captain turned to the Indian who had spoken. Joseph was loading the brass rifle that had been presented to him in England.

The privateer drew alongside.

Joseph looked at John Deseronto. John looked at Joseph Brant. Two rifles were levelled to Mohawk shoulders. Two jets of fire were answered by sharp explosions. Two of the privateer's officers threw up their hands and crumpled to the deck.

This was the signal for general warfare. The crew of the Harriet took up places behind every conceivable object and fired at the disorganized enemy. The privateer came no closer, but hovered within good shooting range. For two hours, the Harriet and the privateer had it out. The battle ended in a draw. The privateer, nursing its wounds, slipped back to sea, while the Harriet limped into a Long Island port near the end of August. She had been over two months on the Atlantic.

Good news met Johnson's party. A terrific battle had been fought on Long Island. General Sullivan and the Continental army had been crushed by the British regulars. Only the coolness and courage of one George Washington had prevented total destruction of the Bostonians. Even now the Commander in Chief of the Continental army was retreating toward White Plains. The British were in possession of the valuable harbor of New York.

There was also bad news for Joseph. In his retreat

from New York, General Washington had blocked the Hudson River Valley. There was no way in which Joseph and John Deseronto could get back to their people with the good news from England.

The Mohawks were forced to cool their heels in New York until late October, when Joseph gained permission from Lord Howe, the British commander, to try to get through the enemy lines. Howe gave his instructions by word of mouth, for he did not want any written messages to be captured. Guy Johnson granted Joseph permission to have a warbelt of wampum made as soon as the Mohawk reached Fort Niagara, and with it to speak in his name.

Brant's companions on this dangerous mission were John Deseronto and Captain Gilbert Tice, formerly the innkeeper at Johnstown. The three men, wearing hunting costumes and coonskin caps and carrying rifles, were rowed across the Hudson near Kingsbridge at night. Once they had passed the Continental lines, they travelled north, skirted the edges of the settlement of Minisink, and plunged into the Catskill Mountains. It was now possible to travel by daylight, for in this thinly-settled region their chief problem was of telling friend from foe. Joseph had been here on hunts and was familiar with the forest trails.

He talked but little during the trip from New York. Even now, as the men approached the settlement of Oquage on the Susquehanna River, he walked silently ahead of his companions. Once he was in sight of the Indian village, he halted.

"Here we are, Gilbert," he announced. "We'll stop here for a day or two before going to the Delaware country."

Tice raised his eyebrows. "Aren't we supposed to go directly to Butler at Niagara?" he asked.

"We'll go to Niagara in due time, but I'm going to talk with the Delawares and the Senecas first."

"But our orders—"

"Gilbert," said Joseph seriously, "you are my friend. A bird has told me that soon my trail will be slippery with blood. This is war, Gilbert. If the Indians go into it, they must go as a united group. It is my duty to unite my people in the cause of the King. That is why I'm going to the Delawares and the Senecas after I have talked with the Mohawks here."

The messengers were received with enthusiasm at Oquage. The Mohawks settled there had been driven from their villages in the Mohawk Valley. They were in desperate need of a leader. And here was Joseph Thayendanegea, back from a visit to the Great White Father over the Great Lake. He could tell them of the wealth of England and inform them about the Great Blue Snake that was Washington's army. Their plows had been bright too long. Their tomahawks needed sharpening. They listened to Joseph with interest and pledged their allegiance to him. They promised to take to the warpath in the spring.

The Delawares and the Senecas also heard Joseph's story. They accepted his leadership and began to put edges on their tomahawks. Joseph was bursting with pride when he arrived at Niagara.

Colonel John Butler received him without enthusiasm.

"The whole Iroquois Confederacy will be ready in the spring," cried Joseph, "but we can't make stew without meat. We need guns and ammunition."

John Butler did not like Joseph. To the colonel, the Mohawk was an upstart who needed to be brought down a peg. "And where will you get it?" he asked.

"You will supply me," was the quick retort.

Butler laughed. "So you are now in command?"

"I'm in command of my people. I am War Chief."

"By whose appointment, may I ask?"

Brant flushed. "My people do not wait for appointments," he countered. "They do not take orders from the Pale Face."

"General Carleton might have something to say about

that. Good day." Butler turned to a message he was writing.

Joseph stood there, his face red, his fingers on his knife. For a shilling he'd bury the blade in that fat chest. Turning on his heel, he left Butler's quarters.

Joseph had the warbelt made. He passed it from tribe to tribe until he had gained the support of the Cayugas, the Senecas and the Mohawks. He invited the Oneidas and the Onondagas to a council near Fort Stanwix. He told them of the wealth of England and pleaded with them to fight for the King. Samuel Kirkland had too much influence there. The Oneida chieftain announced that his people would remain neutral.

Despite this slap, Brant returned to Butler, for he felt sure that the Colonel would not block him again. Butler was still cool. He refused to supply Brant with materials of war. Joseph did not know that General Carleton in Quebec had ordered Butler to clip the wings of the Mohawk Chief.

Chapter XVII

"The Indian Is Free as the Air He Breathes."

WHEN the warm suns came and the death-sheets of snow were turned to streams of water, Joseph Brant summoned the Iroquois to Oquage on the Susquehanna River. The Senecas and the Cayugas, sensing that their future lay in the hands of the Mohawk Chief, sent their warriors in large numbers.

During the Moon of Strawberries eighty warriors appeared at Unadilla. Their leader asked for an interview with Mr. Johnstone, the preacher. The Indian spoke good English.

"I am Joseph Thayendanegea," he told Johnstone and the officers of the militia. "The Pale Face calls me Captain Brant."

"We have heard of you," replied Johnstone coldly. "What is your business with us?"

"I speak for my people. They are hungry. They need cattle and grain."

"Well?" asked Johnstone, stalling for time.

"You have cattle and grain, Mr. Johnstone," came the prompt reply. "If you do not wish to share with us, I fear we shall have to take our portion."

"By force?"

Brant nodded.

"Tell me, Captain Brant, are you for peace or for war?"

"I am concerned with the fate of my people. The Whigs have treated them badly." Brant drew himself to his full height and swept an arm through the air. "The

Mohawks are free as the air they breathe," he cried, "and they are determined to remain so. Your people are holding some of my people prisoners. I demand that you let them go."

"If you are for peace, that could be arranged," replied Johnstone. "But if you are for war—" The preacher shrugged.

Brant stared him down. "The Mohawks have always been warriors," he argued. "They will always be warriors. Their agreement with the King is very strong. They are not such villains as to break it."

"Then it is war. Give us a few hours to think things over. We shall give you an answer by sundown."

When Joseph and his warriors departed for Oquage that evening, they drove ahead of them sheep and cattle. The white inhabitants of Unadilla packed their belongings and headed toward the Mohawk Valley.

General Nicholas Herkimer, in his hip-roofed house beside the Mohawk River, heard the stories of the fleeing settlers. The commanding officer of the Tryon County militia feared no man. He knew Joseph Brant well and respected him. He would talk with the Mohawk Chief and come to an agreement. So he sent Brant a note asking the Indian to meet him at a council in Unadilla.

Captain Brant accepted Herkimer's invitation. He travelled toward Unadilla with five hundred warriors. The late June weather was hot and sultry. Clouds piled up in the western skies each afternoon. Brant advanced slowly, for he wished to have Herkimer cool his heels a few days before the conference. Though he respected the German farmer, he did not trust him. Herkimer had a reputation for shrewdness.

As the Indians approached their objective, Brant sent the half-breed scout, William of Canajoharie, to Herkimer to inquire the reason for the meeting.

"He wants to talk with you," said William.

"He came alone?" Brant wrinkled the corner of one eye.

"He is camped at Unadilla with three hundred militia-men. I asked him if all those men wanted to speak to you, too."

"What did he say?"

"Nothing, so I told him I would take his message to you. I told him not to cross the boundary of his camp."

"You have done well, William. Where will Herkimer meet me?"

"Near that large shed." William pointed to a rude building. "He will leave his guns in camp. He says for you to come unarmed."

Brant frowned. "I shall go tomorrow—unarmed."

Early in the morning he arranged his warriors at the edge of the forest. He would go, but he would also be prepared for treachery. He could see Herkimer and his officers gathering near the shed. Brant had picked his party; it consisted of a Tory leader, the half-breed William of Canajoharie, one woman and forty warriors.

The council circle had formed, with Herkimer and Colonel Ebenezer Cox inside. Joseph Brant and his party entered the circle. He nodded to Herkimer and Cox and sat down cross-legged on the ground.

"Good day, Honnikol," he said to Herkimer. "And what is the reason for thus honoring us?"

Herkimer caught the sarcasm in Brant's tones but he did not show anger. "It is to be a friendly visit between neighbors, Joseph." His accent was thick and guttural. Herkimer spoke German better than he spoke English.

Brant's keen eyes swept the circle. "And all of these have come on a friendly visit, too?" he asked. "All want to see the poor Indians? It is very kind of them." His upper lip curled.

"We want you to come with us to Unadilla."

"I have come far enough."

"Well, we shall talk here. We would like to know your sentiments on the war."

Brant kept his silence.

"Are you with us or with the Tories?" came Herki-mer's next question.

Brant rose to his feet. He pulled his blue blanket around him, but kept his right arm free. "If you must have an answer to that question," he said proudly, "the Indians are in agreement with their King, as their fathers and forefathers have been for many years. The King's belts are yet lodged with us. We cannot and will not violate our pledge. You and your people have joined the Bostonians against your sovereign. The Bostonians may be stubborn, but the King will humble them. The Six Nations have made war on the Pale Face in the past. Then they were united. Now they are divided, but they are not frightened."

Ebenezer Cox rose to his feet and shouted, "If you savages think that way about it, we have nothing more to say to you." His heavy body trembled with anger. His face resembled a ripe beet.

Brant's eyes narrowed. He thought he recognized this man. "Aren't you the son-in-law of George Klock?" he asked.

"Yes," retorted Cox. "What is that to you, you dirty Indian?"

Brant stiffened. With his free arm, he signalled to his warriors. Naked redskins swarmed to the edge of the clearing. Their warwhoops sounded shrill against the forest. Rifles were fired into the air.

"You see," Brant said to Cox, "we are not afraid. I'll go back now."

Herkimer was angry with Cox for his impatience. "Come again tomorrow morning, Joseph," he pleaded. "We will settle this matter."

Brant paused at the edge of the circle. "Very well," he said. "I shall come tomorrow."

The Indians rose at dawn. During the night William of Canajoharie had come in with a report. Herkimer had instructed three of his best marksmen to kill Captain Brant and his chiefs. So the Iroquois were brightening the paint on their bodies and sharpening their tomahawks. If anything happened to their leaders, they were prepared to massacre Herkimer's force.

The Mohawk Chief was the calmest man in camp. He had heard the rumors. They were hard to believe. Nicholas Herkimer had been his neighbor for years. They had fought together against the French and Indians who had threatened their valley. It was strange that this friend should be plotting against him.

Yet not so strange, after all. The Valley was at war. The Pale Faces grasped at each other's throats. Brothers had taken sides against brothers. The white men who called themselves patriots had coaxed the Oneidas and the Tuscaroras away from the Confederacy. Samuel Kirkland had been the chief factor in splitting the Iroquois. And the missionary had been Brant's friend, both at school and in the years that followed. If Kirkland could turn against him, why couldn't Herkimer use treachery to take his life? In time of war men did strange things.

He had two choices. He could go to the council and take a chance on his life or he could turn the Iroquois loose on Herkimer's camp. Such an attack, with forces outnumbering the militia nearly two to one, would result in a wholesale massacre. He would be unable to stop the Senecas, who were complaining about the lack of scalps at their belts.

It would be treachery of the worst sort. Herkimer had come to make peace. At least that was what he had said. If the German general chose to try underhanded methods, that was his business. Joseph Brant would not stoop to similar schemes. But he would not be caught unprepared. The Iroquois would be at the edge of the forest, fully armed, ready to attack at a given signal.

Morning broke calm and sultry. The smoke from hundreds of campfires curled toward a metallic sky. Over the western hills rose banks of clouds sent by Hano, the God of Thunder. Now and then a brilliantly painted warrior would stop to glance at the threatening sky. The Seneca witch doctors were huddled around a fire, seeking for an explanation of the Great Spirit's meaning.

Brant watched them as he ate breakfast. The Senecas,

most western of the Six Nations, had been exposed to Christianity, but they had not accepted its teachings. Even Samuel Kirkland, who had worked wonders with the Oneidas, had failed to convert the Senecas, who were wild as the forest which surrounded them. To be sure, they had learned to cultivate their fields. Great orchards had been planted. The women had done this work. The Seneca warriors lived for one thing and one only, the warpath. Brant was glad he had not turned them loose on Herkimer's militia in the night.

The Mohawk Chief stood at the edge of the forest. A gay blue blanket bordered with red concealed all but his painted face and the cap with the three drooping feathers. He walked boldly across the clearing, followed by William of Canajoharie and a group of warriors. His eyes shifted from side to side, for he suspected that snipers might have rifles levelled at him. The circle had formed. It parted to admit Brant and his warriors. Ebenezer Cox sneered.

"I've come again," said Brant, ignoring Cox, but staring at Herkimer. "The Mohawks have long ears. They have heard about your plans, Honnikol." Herkimer's face flushed at these words. "I am here with my answer. In my quiver is death. My arrows are feathered for blood. They are winged to the winds that find their way in their swift flight. They never come back to me."

He dropped his blanket. His body was painted for the warpath. The red and black lines emphasized his height and the circles around his eyes made the expression on his face frightening. The Mohawk Chief held his head high and lifted his eyes toward the threatening skies. "The Indian is free as the air he breathes," he shouted. "He shall never be a slave to the Pale Face. I have five hundred warriors with me. They are armed and ready for battle. You are in my power, all of you!" From his lips rose the Mohawk war cry, high, piercing, ominous.

The forest became alive with yelling, running figures. Five hundred painted warriors darted into the clearing, dancing, whooping, shooting their rifles into the air. The militiamen tried to form a square to protect themselves, if possible, from a murderous attack.

Joseph Brant held his hand aloft. The warriors disappeared into the forest. The war whoop died away. A streak of lightning parted the clouds. The voice of Hano, the Thunder God, spoke from the distant hills. Hano, riding on his clouds, was destroying monsters who challenged the right of the Iroquois to the land.

The Mohawk Chief was speaking again. "I shall not take advantage of you, Honnikol. We have been friends and neighbors, as you know. But I advise you to go back home. It was nice of you to come to see the poor Indians. Some day they might return the compliment." He picked up his blanket, wrapped it around him, and strode majestically across the clearing, followed by his warriors. He offered an excellent target for any ordinary shot, but no rifle was lifted to a shoulder. He and his warriors disappeared into the forest.

Hano opened his hands. A driving rain drenched the militiamen before they could rush to the shelter of the shed. The West Wind whined like a panther, causing tall trees to sway and creak under its fierce breath. The day became black as night, brightened only by jagged streaks of lightning which cut across the sky. The rumble of Hano's voice against the hills sounded like heavy artillery.

To the Indian and the Pale Face alike, the storm provided an omen of things to come. Night had settled over the Mohawk Valley, a long night filled with agony and vengeance.

Chapter XVIII

"The Indians Must Fight in a Group."

BRANT led his warriors to Lake Ontario. At Oswego he expected to meet Colonel Barry St. Leger, who planned to take Fort Stanwix at the Oneida Carrying Place and march down the Mohawk Valley to make a junction with Howe and Burgoyne at Albany and thus cut off New England from the other colonies.

Two hundred Senecas had gathered at Oswego. Indians were arriving every day. The majority came with no intention of fighting. They planned to watch the British regulars wipe out Fort Stanwix and the settlements. The Indians waited impatiently. Rum was scarce. Ammunition had not been provided. The warriors began to drift away from Oswego. With July on the wane, St. Leger was still twenty miles away.

Daniel Claus arrived with a detachment of soldiers and pitched his tent outside the fort. He had not accompanied St. Leger but had struggled through the northern wilderness. He looked tired and discouraged.

"Good day, Joseph," he said by way of greeting.

They shook hands. Claus waved to a camp stool. Joseph sat on its edge, his back straight as a ramrod.

"How many Indians have you?" Claus asked.

"Eight hundred. I had a thousand."

Claus sighed. "I don't know what's keeping St. Leger. I'm disgusted with the whole affair. The King put me in charge of Indian affairs, yet Butler claims he is the man."

Brant frowned. "I'm sick and tired of Butler, Daniel.

He is just a lickspittle for General Carleton. I talked with
the Six Nations last fall. I stirred them to go on the
warpath. And that fool Butler refused us guns and
ammunition. He and Carleton want to fight this war with
words, like Johnny Burgoyne. Butler should know
better."

"Is Walter with him?" asked Claus.

"Yes, the upstart. He is worse than his father. I hate
him."

There was something in Brant's tones that caused
Claus to stare at the Mohawk Chief. Over Joseph's face
had come an expression that Daniel had never seen there
before. Claus had known the Mohawk at Fort Johnson
and at Johnson Hall. He had seen him often during their
visit to England. On those occasions Joseph had been
calm and mild-mannered. Now he was the redskin on the
warpath. His lips curled away from his teeth. His eyes
shot fire.

"I don't like Walter, either," Claus admitted. "But we
must put up with him and his father, Joseph. After all,
we are fighting in a common cause."

Brant bristled. "Sometimes I wonder about that," he
retorted.

"What do you mean?"

"You know what I mean. The Indians must fight as a
group. They can't be pulled apart. I had them united and
Butler spoiled everything. The Western Indians refused to
come on this expedition. The Oneidas are against us. So
are the Tuscaroras. My sister Molly and my people are in
danger. The Mohawks came here to fight, not to wait.
Our ammunition is low. We are naked and hungry. The
Indian has a simple mind, Daniel. He wants material
things, not promises. I came to you for red paint for our
bodies and powder for our muskets. You will supply me
and my warriors?"

Daniel Claus fingered the hilt of his sword. He had
struggled through the wilderness. There had not been
enough powder to take care of his own small force.
Hunger had cost him several pounds.

Brant understood, but he was not satisfied. "Then you won't do it?" he asked.

"It is not that I won't do it, Joseph. I can't do it. I have neither powder nor paint for your warriors, but I shall send a dispatch to St. Leger right away and ask for them."

Brant rose. "I don't blame you," he said. "But something must be done if I am to hold the Indians. I shall expect results right away or else—" He shrugged and left the tent.

St. Leger arrived the next day with the main army. With him came Johnny Johnson, now Sir John, and the two Butlers. They marched in with pomp and ceremony, to the music of fifes and drums and the jangle of swords. Captain Gilbert Tice was sent to the Indians. He brought them, not powder and red paint, but a quart of rum apiece. The redskins became beastly drunk. They whooped and shrieked all night and slept the following day.

Brant was furious. If Sir William had been alive, the problem would have been handled easily. To be sure, the Irishman's son was with the expedition, but that strutter in scarlet had no power over the Indians. St. Leger meant well. That was all. As for the Butlers, Joseph chose to ignore them. He sulked in his tent.

Daniel Claus came to him. Sir William's son-in-law had slept long. He was shaved and powdered. "I have been to St. Leger," he told Brant. "Lieutenant Bird went forward several days ago, as you know."

Brant nodded. What had this to do with his problem?

"A messenger just came in," Claus explained. "Bird is having the devil's own time with the Indians. St. Leger told him to invest Fort Stanwix but not to attack. The Indians are all for massacring the garrison but they are afraid of the cannon."

A frown creased Brant's forehead. The British despised his warriors because they fought from tree to tree instead of taking chances in the open field.

"Bird can't keep them together," Claus went on.

"They keep wandering off in small parties, looking for victims. Two of them came in with the scalps of two young girls yesterday. St. Leger did not like that, Joseph."

"Ugh, why doesn't he do something about it?"

"That's exactly why I'm here. St. Leger orders you to join Bird with your Mohawks right away. He has heard that batteaux with supplies are coming up the Mohawk River. He wants you to capture them."

"Without ammunition? Would St. Leger have the cowardly Indians fight cannon with tomahawks?"

"I settled that. You will be well supplied. You can start right away?"

On the first of August, a hot sultry day, two hundred Indians, newly painted and well-equipped with powder, left Oswego. Captain Brant, wearing a hunting shirt over his painted body, walked at their head. Behind him trailed the Mohawks and their allies. Their careless manner of advancing caused Barry St. Leger to shake his head. But he could not help but admire the speed with which they advanced up the river toward Oswego Falls.

Batteaux awaited them at Oneida Lake. By nightfall the Indians had reached the blockhouse where Wood Creek emptied its muddy water into the lake. Dawn had not appeared before Brant pushed forward. He ignored the crooked waters of Wood Creek, which had been blocked by fallen trees. His warriors scarcely stirred a leaf as they advanced through the forest. The sun was dropping in the west when they reached the clearing before Fort Stanwix.

A peculiar sight met their eyes. Men were hurrying back and forth between the fort and the Upper Landing Place on the Mohawk River. Several loaded sledges, drawn by perspiring horses, were entering the fort. From the river rose the pat-pat of musketry. All was clear to Brant. The batteaux had arrived. The supplies were being transferred to the fort by the garrison.

The Mohawks hurried to join Bird and his small force.

The last line of soldiers was approaching the fort, with sharpshooters protecting it. Brant had arrived too late! The captain of the batteaux remained at his post, though bullets were spattering around him, making sure that everything was right before he made a dash for the fort. The Mohawks took their revenge upon him. With a whoop and a shriek, a painted warrior dashed out of the woods, followed by several of his tribesmen. They surrounded the captain, who offered feeble resistance. In a few minutes they were shouting the scalp yell against the rampart of Fort Stanwix. The captain lay in the bottom of a batteau. His bleeding head drooped. Red trickled from a knife wound in his chest.

Brant and the Indians camped near the river. There was nothing to do but wait for St. Leger and the main army. The Mohawks amused themselves by taking pot shots at trees and stray animals. At nightfall they would creep into the clearing before the fort. Rifle barks would be followed by shrill yells. There were no replies from the ramparts. Brant sensed that the Bostonians were saving their ammunition while his braves were blowing theirs into thin air, but he made no effort to stop his followers. Give an Indian a gun and he would waste ammunition as fast as he could load the muzzle.

Chapter XIX

"It Is Always the Pale Face Who Is Being Protected."

THE main army appeared on Sunday, August third. The trip from Oswego had proved difficult, for the Bostonians had cluttered Wood Creek with fallen timbers. St. Leger had left his heavy artillery behind. The cocky colonel despised the "rebels". He considered that a mere show of British arms would force Stanwix to surrender. He had no sooner arrived when he ordered the army to parade before the fort.

Joseph Brant smiled to himself. Little did St. Leger know of the courage which lay beneath the coats of the garrison. Brant had lived with these men. He had helped them to beat back invasions from Canada. Fort Stanwix would not be taken by a mere exhibition of strength.

The fort had been silent during the night. Dawn caught it now, lying squat and not quite square on a slight rise above the river. Stanwix was not a thing of beauty. Any European officer would have laughed at it. The piled logs had been thrown together hastily. The pickets rose crude and uneven. And, more amusing than anything else, the stupid Bostonians had erected barracks outside the fort. St. Leger and his officers enjoyed a hearty laugh.

The sun slanted over the trees. Men appeared on the ramparts of the fort. They looked out at the enemy, as if they were welcoming friends. They laughed and joked with each other.

A bugle sounded. The men snapped to attention. They faced the southwest bastion, where several soldiers busied themselves around a rude staff.

100

"They're raising a flag," laughed Sir John Johnson, his broad shoulders shaking. Colonel Butler joined in the hilarity.

As the flag rose clumsily to the top of the staff, the breeze caught its folds and revealed to the besieging army a banner of red, white and blue. Its stripes were uneven. The white strips in the blue field meant nothing to the British. But the men of the fort split their throats with cheers at sight of an emblem which meant more to them than the British could possibly understand. St. Leger would live to recognize the spirit behind that crude banner. So would Sir John Johnson and Colonel John Butler. *For the new flag of the United States of America was being flown for the first time by an American fort under siege by an enemy!*

Joseph Brant stood at the head of his painted warriors. He may have seen significance in this event. If he did, he gave no sign. His face, decorated for the warpath, did not move a muscle.

Drums rolled. Fifes shrilled. Orders flew. In lines of scarlet, the British regulars marched along the edge of the forest. The sun, released from the trees, flashed against the polished bayonets and burnished the braid on the officers' hats. Regimental flags, unpacked that morning, waved above the heads of the marching soldiers. The Hessians, surly of face and heavy of step, followed the regulars. Despite the summer weather, they wore their long green coats with scarlet trimmings. Their muskets were pressed against their shoulders. Johnson's Greens, poorly equipped and imperfectly drilled, brought up the rear.

More suited to the occasion were Brant's Indians, who danced ahead of the regulars, on the flanks, in the rear, their painted bodies writhing and twisting, their voices raised in blood-curdling yells.

The regulars and the Hessians passed the fort. Distance silenced the shrilling fifes. Only the muffled tread of feet accompanied the thundering drums as the British moved to their camp to the east of the fort. Johnson and his

Greens wheeled and returned to the river, escorted by
the shrieking Indians. Here they would camp in order to
cut off any possible connection between Fort Stanwix
and the Mohawk River.

At three o'clock the drums rolled. Captain Gilbert
Tice went into the fort under a flag of truce, carrying
with him a proclamation by the hand of General Burgoyne. He returned crestfallen. Colonel Peter Gansevoort,
Commandant of Fort Stanwix, had refused point-blank
to surrender. The siege was on.

Night fell. Brant's Indians slipped from camp to duck
under the walls of the fort and take shots at the sentries.
They circled the square structure and shouted their
defiance into the heavy air. A cannon charged with grape
killed one redskin and caused the rest to scatter.

Joseph Brant had his eye on the barracks outside the
fort. On Tuesday he sent a band of Mohawks across the
clearing. They reached the barracks and set them afire.
The smoke drifted into the fort and almost smothered
the garrison. The Indians rushed toward the ramparts.
Once more it took a charge of grape to drive them away.

Brant watched the performance from a distance. It
seemed useless to him. How on earth did St. Leger
expect to besiege a fort with whooping Indians? Why
didn't he bring up some siege machinery? Daniel Claus
supplied the answer. St. Leger had left the big guns in
Oswego.

Night set in, hot and heavy. The Indians were celebrating the burning of the barracks by warming their
insides with rum. Whoops and yells rang along the river.
The fort remained silent.

Joseph Brant could not sleep. He slipped out of his
tent and walked to the river. The Mohawk lay silvery
and peaceful. Lightning-bugs sparkled against the forest
in feeble imitation of the stars. A solitary frog croaked
in the marshland.

Here lay the primeval wilderness, the land that had
been given to the Indian by the Great Spirit. Here he

was to hunt and to fish, to go on the warpath, to live the carefree life he loved. And yet, less than a half mile away, loomed the gray shadow of civilization. Fort Stanwix had been built to protect the Mohawk Valley. Against whom? The British had told Brant it was to protect the Indians against the French. Now the Bostonians insisted it was to guard against the British who had built it.

Brant sat down on a log and stretched his legs before him. His gay blanket hung loosely over his shoulders, revealing his painted body. "Strange," he told himself, "the Pale Face is forever protecting something. And it is always the Pale Face who is being protected. The French said they were protecting the Indians. The British told us they were protecting our lands. But for whom? For the Pale Face. The British and the French were both protecting our lands so that they could grab all they wanted. And now the Bostonians were doing the same thing. We are fighting for the King. He has made great promises. I wonder."

He sat upright as a sound in the bushes caught his ears.

"Joseph, where are you?" called a voice.

"Here."

Captain Gilbert Tice appeared. "I have a note for you," he said. "A runner just came through with it. It is from your sister."

Brant sprang to his feet and took the note. "Let me read it, Gilbert," he said. He ran toward the camp.

Tice watched him read the note in the light of a fire. He saw Joseph's jaw set.

"The time has come," Brant told him. "Molly has received information that Herkimer and twelve hundred militiamen are marching up the Valley to raise the siege. They are to camp on the other side of Oriska Creek tonight. Come, we must plan to meet them in the morning."

Chapter XX

"Oo-nah! Oo-nah!"

SIX miles east of Fort Stanwix a brook rushed from
the uplands toward the Mohawk. A mile from that
river, it tumbled over logs and stones into a deep ravine.
This V-shaped hollow had been carved out of the rocks
centuries before, when the stream had been a river or at
least a creek. Here the water paused, as if amazed that
its progress could be blocked. It lay in pools between
hummocks of rank grass except for a small stream which
meandered through the ravine toward the river.

A road descended from the east, spanned the brook
with a rude bridge and wandered up the western slope
toward the fort. This military highway from Albany to
Oswego was not much more than a path through the
forest. Its ruts, though hard and dry on the slopes, were
filled with oozy mud nearer the brook. On either side of
the log bridge pools of water made the road part of the
swamp. A canopy of trees provided shade that was damp
and forbidding, like the coldness of death.

Joseph Brant had crossed this ravine many times; so
had Sir John Johnson and Colonel Butler. The spot was
ideal for an ambush. If Herkimer could be caught in its
depths, it would not be difficult to defeat his forces,
even to wipe them out. Barry St. Leger listened carefully
to Brant, to Johnson and to Butler. The refusal of
Colonel Gansevoort to surrender Fort Stanwix had upset
St. Leger's plans. He was willing to grasp at any straw
which might speed his progress down the Mohawk Valley. He refused to send his regulars, however. Sir John

and his Greens, together with Brant's whooping Indians,
might do the job better. St. Leger chose to wait in camp
for news of their victory.

Five hundred Indians, trembling with excitement, hurried out of camp that night. Brant had warned them
against whooping. They obeyed his order. No similar
force ever advanced more quietly. The Indians were
stripped for action. Warpaint, feathers and breechclouts
were their only clothing. Their guns were loaded. Tomahawks and knives decorated their belts. The few braves
left behind kept the fires burning, thus fooling the sentries on the ghostly fort. The redskins moved along the
military road swiftly. Johnson's Greens and Butler's
Rangers marched behind them; their steps imitated
clumsily the noiseless tread of the Indians.

Dawn met them at the ravine. Herkimer had not
arrived. There was time to prepare the ambush.

Sir John Johnson came to Brant. "We should give our
friend Honnikol a merry reception," he told the
Mohawk. His face wore a pleased expression.

Brant shrugged. He never counted his chickens before
they were hatched. Herkimer was a shrewd man. He
would not ride into a trap with his eyes closed. If
Ebenezer Cox were leading the relief party, the task
would be simple. That blundering fool would rush headlong into an ambush. But Honnikol was another man.

The Indians were restless. They longed to take shots at
squirrels which chattered in the bushes or to risk some
powder on the crows which cawed from a dead oak on
the heights.

Sir John watched them. "You told them not to shoot
until the signal comes?" he asked Brant.

The Mohawk Chief nodded. He had told them, yes,
but that was no sign they would obey. He touched the
silver whistle which hung from a cord around his neck.
"When I blow three times," he said, "they shoot. Not
until then—I hope."

He called William of Canajoharie. The Scout's face was

shining. William had many deals to settle. "Take places
on both sides of the road," Brant ordered him. "And
keep well back, behind the trees and bushes. Three blasts
of my whistle is the signal, as you know. Don't let a
man shoot before that signal."

The Indians blended with the forest. No sound rose
from the ravine. No breeze stirred the beeches, birches
and maples. The hemlocks stood straight and green as a
tardy sun climbed over them. Oppressive heat replaced
the coolness of dawn. Locusts droned their endless tunes,
but no bird sang. Mating season was long past and this
was no morning for singing.

Sir John smiled his approval. "I'll station my men on
high ground, Joseph" he remarked. "We'll give Honnikol
a real reception if he tries to climb the western slope.
Some of my men have old affairs to settle this morning.
It should be fun."

A Mohawk warrior appeared as if by magic. "They are
coming," he said, "along the road from Oriska Creek.
They should be here any minute."

"Who's leading them?" snapped Brant.

"Cox is riding at the head with the Canajoharie men,
then Klock and Honnikol. Visscher is in the rear." The
Mohawk stared at Brant. "I want Cox," he said.

"At my signal."

The Mohawk Chief watched from the western slope of
the ravine. He stood motionless, his lips parted, his ears
tuned to the sounds of the forest.

A low rumbling caught his ears. Nearer and nearer it
came until he knew it to be the tramp of feet and the
shouts of human beings. Laughs and oaths rose above the
conversation. The eastern slope became alive with sound,
in striking contrast to the deathly silence of the ravine.
Brant, watching closely, could see a painted head bob up
occasionally from the undergrowth and disappear as suddenly as it had risen. It became clear to him that Herkimer had sent out no scouts. The German general would
lead his army into the ambush.

A horseman appeared where the rutted road began its descent toward the brook. It was Ebenezer Cox, his heavy figure astride a farm horse, his face florid. With the sleeve of his coat, he wiped the perspiration from his brow. The Mohawk crouching beside Brant raised his rifle to his shoulder. His chief pushed it down. The warrior raised inquiring eyes. Brant shook his head. "Not yet," he hissed.

Cox rode forward. His horse picked its way carefully, as if unwilling to enter the ravine. The man from Canajoharie struck its flanks with his sword. The animal whinnied a protest but advanced toward the brook. The militiamen followed. Their guns were slung over their shoulders. Their make-shift uniforms were caked with dust and stained with sweat.

They saw the brook! Paying no attention to their leader, they swept past Cox toward the inviting water. Stretching out on their bellies, they drank the coolness which satisfied their thirst. Cox, yelling and cursing, tried to get them to move on. Their smiles defied him. More men staggered down the road, more horsemen. The brook was their goal. Klock's regiment also wanted to share the refreshment. Carts rumbled down the slope. They found their way barred by the thirsty militiamen. The forest echoed to the angry cries of men who thought only of themselves in this fierce desire to reach the water.

A white horse was fighting its way through the crowd. Its rider, a stocky German, was trying to bring order out of chaos.

"It's Honnikol," Brant muttered. "Cox has got him into a mess this time."

That red-faced colonel, through curses and pleading, had whipped his troops into some kind of order. The Canajoharie regiment began to climb the western slope, followed by Klock's men. Drums sounded on the eastern heights. Visscher, with the rear guard, was preparing to enter the trap. Once he started down the decline, the

ambush would be complete. Joseph Brant fingered his
silver whistle.

The Mohawk warrior had been watching his chief. He
saw Brant's hands move. Raising his gun to his shoulder,
he levelled it at the broad chest of Ebenezer Cox. A
sharp crack resounded through the forest. Cox rose in his
stirrups, gave one shriek of agony, and toppled off his
horse.

Brant cursed the Mohawk, who was already running
through the undergrowth toward his victim. Pressing the
whistle to his lips, he blew three shrill blasts.

The forest became alive with naked bodies and flashes
of orange. The militiamen, stunned by this sudden attack
by unseen foes, stood in their tracks. Those that were
drinking at the brook raised inquiring eyes. Some of
them, stung by the accuracy of Indian aim, let their
heads sink into the cool water. Others clutched at their
sides and struggled to drag themselves to safety.

A white horse screamed and staggered into the bushes.
Two militiamen were pulling General Herkimer from
beneath its carcass. Honnikol's legs were dragging along
the ground. His face was pale as death. Colonel Visscher,
trying to rally his forces, put a hand to his face. He
wheeled his horse and galloped toward the east.

All was confusion in the hollow. The militiamen,
deprived of their leaders, fought as frontiersmen. It was
each man for himself and the devil take the hindmost.
Their rifles barked from behind trees, fallen logs, bodies
of comrades. This method of fighting pleased the
Indians. Their painted bodies hurried through the undergrowth. Tomahawks flashed before descending with dull
thuds. Hideous scalpyells rent the air. A wave of green
straggled down the western slope. Johnson's Tories were
sweeping into the ravine to take revenge on their neighbors. Complete victory seemed at hand.

Joseph Brant threw himself headlong into the struggle.
He seemed to be everywhere at the same time. His
tomahawk flashed. His blood-spattered body leaped from

tree to tree. He was no longer a leader. He was one more Indian, fighting hand to hand with the men who were his enemies. His forces were completely out of control.

Opposed to Brant was one of the shrewdest brains in the Mohawk Valley. Nicholas Herkimer's leg had been shattered, but his mind was still active. The militiamen had dragged their leader up the western slope. Here he sat, under a tree, his pipe glowing between lips that were gray. Orders came from his throat, guttural barks which were obeyed by his despairing comrades. The militiamen stopped their individual fighting. Knots sprang together. Bands of tough farmers charged into the underbrush.

Shrieks burst from Indian throats. The redskins had no stomach for this kind of fighting. They began to slink away, one by one. Colonel Visscher and the rear guard were on the run. It was far more exciting to chase them than it was to stand up before the determined advances of the men in the ravine.

Brant saw what was happening. He rushed madly to and fro. He cursed. He pleaded. It was no use. The Senecas were already running up the eastern slope. Their rapid strides were gaining on Visscher's heavy-footed farmers. Horses made easy targets. The Senecas shrieked with pleasure as they watched the death agonies of these beasts of burden.

Dark clouds had covered the sun, thus adding to the gloom of the blood-spattered ravine. The warwhoops faded toward the east. Only the cries of the wounded rose from the marshlands near the brook. The reorganized militiamen were backing up the western slope toward General Herkimer. Their rifles sprayed the bushes in the hope of catching an Indian. Johnson's Greens melted into the forest.

There was nothing Joseph Brant could do about it. He who had said that the Indians were free as the air they breathed could understand fully the meaning of that statement. The Pale Face had learned some organization. In time of need it had brought results. The Indian had refused to take orders. The effects of that freedom could be seen.

Brant climbed toward higher ground. If and when his Indians returned from their pursuit of Visscher, they might be persuaded to attack Herkimer. That he doubted, for his men hated fighting in the open field.

A distant sound caught his ears. Three dull reports came from the west. It was the cannon from Fort Stanwix. Was St. Leger attacking? Brant did not think so. But is was all puzzling, very puzzling.

Sir John Johnson poured out his disappointment to Brant.

Joseph took it without twitching a muscle. "You should know Indians by now, Johnny," he said. "They will fight like fiends while things are going well. They fought nobly in the ravine. Honnikol was too clever for us. That is the answer."

Indians were straggling back. They came with a few scalps and some booty. Visscher had been put completely to rout. His men were running madly down the Mohawk Valley. Many braves did not return. Their bodies lay in the ravine. William of Canajoharie was among them. A counting of noses discouraged the Senecas, who had lost most heavily. They told Brant they wouldn't fight any more. They had come to watch St. Leger trounce the settlers. Instead, he and his precious regulars had remained in camp while the Indians had done the fighting.

"You see?" asked Brant. "It's no use now, Johnny."

Sir John was stubborn. He was proud. "I'm disguising my men as militiamen," he said. "They are going toward Herkimer as friends and then cut the farmers to pieces."

"Ugh," grunted Joseph, who was not convinced that Herkimer would be fooled.

Further discussion was interrupted by a torrent of rain. The clouds seemed to open and the whole heavens to drop to earth. There was nothing to do but wait. The rain lasted an hour. It cooled brows that had been hot and perspiring. It also washed off the ardor of men who had marched to battle with so much enthusiasm.

Johnson's Greens made their move in mid-afternoon. Herkimer's men rushed to meet them. Terrific hand-to-hand fighting followed. Here neighbor slew neighbor while Brant and his Indians watched the Pale Face slaughter each other. The Greens were badly beaten. Many lay dead in the gulley. The others turned tail and ran for the heights.

"Oo—nah! Oo—nah!"

Joseph Brant forgot his silver whistle. His chest rose and fell as his throat poured out the retreat call of the Mohawks.

The Indians took the road to Fort Stanwix. Some of them limped badly. Others pressed hands to bleeding wounds. Cries of mourning rose for warriors who would never return. Behind them marched Johnson's Greens, a discouraged lot of soldiers.

A Mohawk runner met the party two miles from the fort. He rushed up to Captain Brant. "Come quick," he gasped. "The men from the fort are attacking our camp. They are taking our blankets and our kettles."

Brant spurred his tired Indians forward. They reached the plain near the river too late. Their camp was completely destroyed. Tents had been toppled. Blankets, kettles, food, and clothing were gone. Several dead warriors lay stretched out on the ground, together with a few redcoats. None of them had been scalped.

A great wailing rose from the Indians. They had come on this expedition to see St. Leger beat the Bostonians. Instead, the British colonel and his regulars had remained in camp while the Indians had fought and died. A bitterness settled over the redskins who sat shivering around the fires. The Indian liked to be naked in battle. He fought better that way. But he did not enjoy camping with an empty stomach and shivering shoulders.

Brant did not wait to see their discomfort. He went to St. Leger. There was only one thing to do; that was to

dash down the Mohawk Valley and wreck the settlements before the militiamen could recover from the blow
at Oriskany.

St. Leger could not see it that way. "I am opposed to
wholesale slaughter." he told the Mohawk Chief. "This is
a humane war."

Brant bristled. "How can war be humane?" he argued.
"How can you make rules when the end is for one man
to kill another? I saw my men murdered this morning,
murdered by those same people you want to spare. My
people seek only one thing. That is revenge. We could
wipe out every settlement between here and Schenectady. Leave Stanwix where it is. What harm can it do
after we join Burgoyne at Albany?"

"You don't see the situation clearly, Captain Brant,"
said St. Leger, who seemed undisturbed by the Mohawk's
anger. "We must take Stanwix first. In war an officer
cannot leave his supply lines blocked by a fort."

"Break the rules for once," Brant retorted. "Take a
chance, man, and victory will be ours."

St. Leger would not budge. He remained before Fort
Stanwix, sending bombastic notes and firing weak can-
non at the log ramparts. Brant's Indians became unruly.
It was all he could do to keep them from straggling
away. Some of them did. Rum was no substitute for
clothing and food. Brant was glad when news came that
General Benedict Arnold and a Continental army were
coming to the relief of the fort. That fool, Hon Yost
Schuyler, had brought the message. He had made St.
Leger believe that the Yankees would outnumber the
British three to one. Brant knew better. Molly had written him that Arnold's force was not much larger than
that of St. Leger. He told the British colonel, but that
individual, sure that the jig was up, pulled stakes and
retreated toward Oswego.

The Indians did not know what to do. Brant, opposed
to retreating, gathered his Mohawks around him.
Together they would make a dash down the Valley

toward Albany. The Senecas and the other Indians stayed with St. Leger. Their time was spent in stealing clothes and muskets from British regulars. They murdered a few for the sport of the thing.

Brant swept toward Albany with a handful of the faithful Mohawks. He released captives from Mohawk villages. He caught up with Burgoyne near Saratoga. When the trees shed their leaves and the fur of the elk grew long, he left the British army and returned to Niagara.

Chapter XXI

"I Had to Shoot."

JOSEPH Brant could see beyond the end of his nose. Winning the war was important, but what would be the Indian's place in peace? Would he be a free man or would he find himself under the heel of the Pale Face, regardless which side won the war?

Joseph spent much time at Niagara trying to organize an Indian Confederacy. He mentioned the subject to Colonel John Butler, who told him to mind his own business. The harder Brant worked, the more obstacles seemed to get in his way. It wasn't only Butler and the Pale Faces who opposed his idea. Other leaders of his own people also blocked him.

Cornplanter, that half-breed son of a Dutch trader and a Seneca woman, thought that the Indians could be saved only through taking sides with the Bostonians. Cornplanter had visited Continental army leaders. He was holding councils in Indian villages: Brant liked Cornplanter. The half-breed was brave on the warpath and fair in his negotiations, but he betrayed a lack of vision by splitting the Indians at a time when their strength lay in unity.

For Red Jacket, that upstart who was neither a chief nor a warrior, Brant held only contempt. The little Seneca, whose tongue was his warclub, kept dropping poison on dissatisfied minds. Many Senecas had fallen at Oriskany. Their bodies lay rotting in the ravine near the swampy brook. They had died while the redcoats rested in camp before Fort Stanwix. True, the Senecas had gained some revenge during the retreat toward Canada. A few scalps and some bright uniforms had been taken. That was all. They opened their ears to Red Jacket's oratory. The greater cause that Brant preached was more than their minds could understand.

It took a woman to straighten out the difficulties. Molly Brant was wintering in a Cayuga village. Joseph went to his sister. She listened to his troubles.

"Joseph," she told the Mohawk Chief, "you have been long among white men. Your mind grasps ideas which are far removed from the primitive thoughts of our people. The Seneca lives from day to day. If he is hungry, he hunts game. If he is naked, he throws a skin over his shoulders. If he is in love, he finds a wife. If he is wronged, he sulks."

"Sulking won't get the Senecas anywhere now," protested Joseph.

"Neither will bullying." Molly held up a hand. "The Senecas are great warriors. They have not felt the hand of the Pale Face. You were brought up with white people, Joseph. You are no Seneca. It is natural that they should be jealous of your leadership."

"But I am thinking of them as well as of the Mohawks."

"I know, Joseph, but they aren't sure of you. That's why they listen to Red Jacket." Molly's lip curled with a woman's scorn for a coward. "You are a man and a warrior. The Senecas are jealous of you. But," she added, narrowing one eye, "if they are used to taking advice from women, maybe they would listen to me."

Joseph grasped the point. Molly was much respected among the Senecas and the Cayugas. He did not argue further.

"You go to Oquage or Unadilla or whatever place you are planning to make your headquarters," Molly told him. "I'll see that the Senecas and the Cayugas send warriors. I shall also keep the loud mouths away."

The Cornplanting Moon found Joseph at Unadilla

fortifying the settlement. Seven hundred painted warriors
had arrived. Cornplanter and Red Jacket stayed away.
Molly had done her work well.

Captain Bob McKean of Cherry Valley, with a handful
of fellow-residents, crossed through the woods to look
over Brant's position. He approached within twenty-five
miles and stopped at a stone house. Here he learned that
Indians had gathered in great numbers and were fortifying Unadilla. In fact, Brant himself had appeared at the
house that very morning and would return by nightfall.

McKean wanted to wait and give the Indians a merry
reception. His men possessed less daring but more common sense. They chose to go home.

"Very well," said the captain from Cherry Valley, "I'll
go home with you, but I'll leave a little note for
Joseph."

When Brant returned that evening, the message
awaited him. He read the crude writing with eyes that
blazed. McKean had called him a traitor and a snake. He
had challenged him to single combat in an open field. If
Brant would come to Cherry Valley, McKean would
change the Mohawk's name from Brant to goose.

These insulting words made Joseph burn all over. He
liked Bob McKean. He respected McKean's ability. But
no man could say such things about the Mohawk War
Chief and expect him to swallow them.

The first blow fell immediately. With fifty warriors, he
swooped down upon Springfield at the head of Otsego
Lake, sometimes called Glimmerglass. The attack caught
the settlers by surprise. Several men were captured. All
houses but one were burned. Into this remaining structure he herded the women and children. Not a hair of
their heads was touched.

He hurried east toward Cherry Valley. The appletrees
had burst in full bloom, while the ground was pink with
dying cherry blossoms. Here and there the rolling fields
had been broken by the plow. Wisps of smoke rose from
piles of burning brush.

He paused to stare at figures moving in the fields. They created tiny flashes of color against the green forest. These people knew he lurked in the neighborhood. They appreciated the horrors which an Indian attack could bring, yet they continued to cultivate their land. There was something pathetic about them, yet something so courageous that Brant could not help but admire them. He did not bother these isolated settlers. He could deal with them later. Cherry Valley was his goal. He'd show Bob McKean who was the goose.

Dusk was falling as the Indians reached the heights overlooking the settlement. Smoke from burning brush clung close to the soil, blending with a mist which rose from the lowlands. A cluster of houses huddled around the fort like chicks seeking the warmth and protection of their mother's feathers.

Joseph Brant shaded his eyes with his hand. What were those ants moving around in the front of the fort? They marched in formation along the parade ground, wheeled, and retraced their course. A Springfield prisoner had told Brant that Cherry Valley was being reinforced by a Massachusetts regiment. The Chief hadn't believed him. These settlers had a way of misleading him with false information. Yet, at the limit of his vision, he could see figures drilling in the dusk. His Indians saw them, too. To risk an attack would be folly. To take the fort would be impossible. Brant was angry with himself. Why hadn't he left Unadilla with a larger force?

He saw two larger insects detach themselves from the swarm. Brant awoke with a start. These were horsemen riding toward the Mohawk Valley. He could cut them off and worm from them the required information. The Indians hurried toward the trail, dragging their Springfield prisoners with them. A deep glen opened before them. Here they waited.

Hoofs thundered along the rude road. Two horsemen appeared. Brant recognized them as men from Fort Plain. Matt Wormuth was more than a neighbor; he was a

friend of long standing. Peter Sitz was a mere acquaint-
ance. The men were riding rapidly. Their eyes searched
the woods on either side of the road.

Brant had ordered his men not to shoot. He wanted
information and dead men do not talk. As Wormuth and
Sitz entered the narrow glen, he blew a shrill blast on his
whistle. Indians rushed into the road. One horse stopped
short, throwing its rider over its head. Peter Sitz lay face
down in the bushes.

Wormuth was made of sterner stuff. Crouching low
against his horse's neck, he dug his spurs into the meaty
flanks. The animal shrieked and rushed headlong down
the trail. Two Indians were bowled over in the mad rush.
Others scurried for safety.

Joseph Brant's gun went to his shoulder. Matt Wormuth had been his friend. He was a brave fellow, to be
sure. But Sitz lay like dead in the path. Brant would
pink Wormuth in the shoulder and bring him down. His
gun barked. Wormuth's horse crashed into the bushes. Its
rider dropped to the ground like a sack of meal. The
Mohawk Chief hurried to his victim and knelt beside
him.

Wormuth lay mortally wounded. The bullet had drilled
him through. He opened his eyes. For a second or two,
they grasped nothing. Then they filled with horror. Wormuth's lips moved. "It's you," said the dying man.

"Yes, Matt. I didn't mean to kill you. I wanted information and you tried to get away. I had to shoot."

Wormuth was slipping fast. "Let me die, you savage,"
he muttered. Blood frothed at his lips.

Brant grasped him by the shoulder. "Are the Massachusetts men at the fort?" he demanded.

"I—wouldn't—tell—you—nothin'." Wormuth's head
dropped on his chest.

Brant lost control of himself. He shook his victim
fiercely. Wormuth's body yielded to the punishment, for
life had gone from it. Brant had come miles to get this
information. This man had denied it to him.

Joseph saw red. He was no longer the educated man. He was Joseph Thayendanegea, a Mohawk Chief on the warpath. Seizing Wormuth by the hair, he slipped his knife around the scalp and ripped it loose. A chorus of approving grunts rose from the watching Senecas.

Sitz was not dead. He answered Brant's question. "Sure," he said wearily, "the fort's got enough men to beat off three hundred savages."

Chapter XXII

"My Name Is Brant!"

THERE was bigger business on hand than attacking Cherry Valley. Colonel John Butler was marching south with a large band of Tories and Indians. His goal was Wyoming in Pennsylvania, that settlement of arguing Pale Faces. He would put an ened to their squabbles. Brant had orders to attack Cobleskill. The fort there was undermanned. It should be easy to wipe out the small force and ravage the whole Schoharie Valley.

Brant planned the attack on Cobleskill carefully. By sending ahead twenty or thirty Indians, he coaxed the garrison into the forest. The trick worked beautifully. Outnumbered and outmaneuvered, the militiamen tried to retreat, but were cut down by the accurate fire from the undergrowth. A running fight followed, with both sides shooting from behind trees and logs. A few of the garrison succeeded in returning to the fort. Many others were killed or captured.

In the hand-to-hand fighting, Joseph Brant encountered a young lieutenant, a tall, tough fellow. They both missed with their rifles. Brant rushed at the lieutenant. As he raised his tomahawk for the death blow, he was halted by a sign made by his intended victim. Brant's arm dropped to his side. He had recognized the sign of the Masonic Order.

"Go, Brother," he said, pointing.

The lieutenant vanished into the forest.

Others were not so fortunate. Two soldiers were trapped in an isolated house. The building was set afire and the victims held inside by steady fire until both men were roasted alive, to the glee of the Indians. The Senecas caught and scalped an officer. Into his hand they forced a roll of Continental bills to remind Congress of the uselessness of their promises to pay. Houses were fired. The Senecas danced around them, letting out whoops which terrified survivors who watched from the tower of the fort. Night and rain ended the massacre. The Indians took care of their wounded and buried the few who had been killed. They hastened toward the west, dragging with them prisoners and cattle.

At Unadilla Joseph Brant discovered that John Butler had returned from Wyoming. The entire settlement had been wiped out. The belts of the Senecas were lined with scalps. Butler and his Tories boasted of their achievements. Later they tried to fix the blame on Brant, though he was miles away from Wyoming at the time of the massacre.

It was not until midsummer that Brant learned how Peter Sitz had deceived him at Cherry Valley. He was wandering through the forest alone, as was sometimes his custom. He wanted to see Jacky Foster and Wiggy Wilson, two Tories who lived near Cherry Valley. They often had valuable information.

The Mohawk Chief had recovered from the rage which had resulted in the scalping of Matt Wormuth. He felt quite satisfied with the world as he walked along the path toward Cherry Valley. The hay was being cut in the clearings. Brant thought it fun to watch the unsuspecting farmers taking in their harvest.

A fifteen-year-old boy was tedding hay in a nearby clearing. Brant stopped to watch his lazy handling of the rake. White boys did not like farm work any better than did Indian youngsters. This boy probably would prefer to be splashing in some pool or catching trout in the ripples. Brant permitted himself one of his rare smiles as his catlike steps carried him close behind the youngster.

"Ugh," he grunted.

The boy jumped a foot and wheeled to face the intruder. The rake dropped from his hands. He stood there, pale, helpless, his mouth open.

"Don't be afraid, young man," said Brant. "I shall not hurt you."

The boy wasn't so sure. But what could he do, with this painted warrior standing before him, gun in hand, tomahawk shining from his belt?

"Do you know Jacky Foster?" asked Brant, resting his gun against the trunk of a tree.

This act brought back the lad's confidence. "I know who he be," he replied. "I seen him once to Bowman's Creek."

"What's your name, lad?"

"Bill McKown."

"I know your father. He's Bob McKean's neighbor, isn't he?"

The boy nodded. "You know Bob?" he asked, expectantly.

Brant's face clouded. "I know him well," he answered. "He's a brave man, but he's too cock-sure of himself. I'll meet him again one of these days. Bob and I have some things to settle." His manner changed. "Where will I find Foster?"

The boy gave him directions. At the close he asked, "And who be you?"

The Mohawk Chief hesitated. It occurred to him that he might have some fun with this youngster. Picking up his gun, he answered, "My name is Brant!"

The boy paled. "What!" he gasped. "Captain Brant?"

"No," said the Mohawk Chief, winking one eye at the unhappy lad, "I am a cousin of his." He disappeared into the forest before the boy could recover from his surprise.

Joseph did not find Foster but he met Wiggy Wilson on the outskirts of the settlement. Wiggy told him that reinforcements had come to defend the fort.

"When did they arrive?" Brant asked him.

"Yesterday."

"How many?"

"Three hundred."

"Who's in command?"

"Colonel Ichabod Alden. I saw him last night. He thinks he's quite a feller."

"An Indian fighter?"

Wiggy shook his head in the negative.

"You say they came only yesterday?"

"That's right. I saw 'em come in."

"But Peter Sitz told me—"

"Yeah, I heard about that," said Wiggy, winking slyly.

"But it's all strange. I was down here in late May. Who were the soldiers drilling before the fort? I saw them from that hill," said Brant, pointing. "I didn't get a good look at them."

"Soldiers?" laughed Wiggy. "You must have seen the young lads out drillin', Joseph. They parade every evenin' with their wooden guns. Maybe that's what Pete Sitz was atryin' to tell ye."

"Thanks, Wiggy," said Brant shortly. He didn't wait to hear more. He hadn't liked Wiggy's laughter. Wiggy might be a Tory but he was also a Pale Face. White men enjoyed jokes on Indians. Probably all Cherry Valley would know by tomorrow how the Mohawk Chief had been fooled by youngsters on parade.

Chapter XXIII

"I Have Never Made War on Women and Children."

OCTOBER was cold and blowy. The ground was frozen by the middle of the month. Light snow lay where it had fallen. Brant and his warriors, poorly equipped for this kind of weather, hurried along the trail to the lake country. Their moccasins slipped and slid where the sun had loosened the frost-bitten soil. Joseph was disappointed. So were his braves. The Senecas felt that the campaign had not brought enough in scalps and booty. They would return to their villages, where Red Jacket would talk to them all winter.

They were nearing Cayuga Lake when a messenger rushed up to Brant. He carried important news. Walter Butler and two hundred Tory rangers were marching from Niagara. Butler sent orders from his father. Brant was to wait for Walter and join him in an attack upon Cherry Valley.

Brant's first thought was to send the messenger back to Butler with a refusal. Who did these Butlers think they were, anyway? If they were so anxious to attack Cherry Valley, why hadn't they come before snow and cold weather made the task more difficult?

Why was young Walter Butler in command? He knew nothing of warfare. Colonel Butler's son had been captured by General Benedict Arnold at the German Flatts the year before. He had recently escaped from captivity in Albany. Was this attack being made merely to satisfy Walter's desire for revenge? If so, Brant wanted nothing to do with it. Cherry Valley had held out all summer. He had many friends there. He did not mind killing settlers but he hated to spill blood to satisfy the Butlers.

The Seneca chiefs, hearing the news, asked for a council. They were for turning back. Together with Butler's force, they could sweep down on Cherry Valley and surprise the settlers. More scalps and plunder would strengthen their positions at home. Brant listened to the chiefs, knowing in his heart that if he refused them his policy would be criticized by Red Jacket. He might lose the support of the Senecas and thus ruin any chance he might have for uniting the Six Nations under his leadership.

Butler came up the next day, swelling with importance. "Good day, Joseph," he said by way of greeting. He put out a hand which the Mohawk ignored. "Very well," said Butler, his swarthy cheeks a dull red, "if you want to take that attitude, well and good. It makes no difference to me. I am in command of this expedition and you will do as I say."

Butler's green uniform served to emphasize the fact that the lawyer was no soldier. Walter wore no wig. His long black hair fringed a face which betrayed in its thin nose and lips the meanness of the man. His eyes shifted from side to side. With his tapering fingers, he fidgeted at the gold cord of his coat.

"You're quite a fellow, aren't you, Butler?" asked Brant with withering scorn.

"Never mind the insults," retorted Butler. "We have a job to do. If you're afraid to turn back, I think I can persuade the Senecas to go without you."

"Did you say afraid?" Brant's hand went to his tomahawk.

Butler shrugged. "We march this afternoon."

A smile of superiority parted his thin lips. "Good day, Joseph."

Joseph avoided Butler all the way to Cherry Valley. He convinced himself that this attack was being made to satisfy Walter's blood-thirsty desire for fame. The Indians would be the tools by which Butler would forge his success.

He decided to block Butler. At a council held near the outskirts of the settlement, he brought up the fact that several families in Cherry Valley should be spared. Mr. Dunlop, the aged preacher, could do no harm. Robert Wells, though a Whig, had always dealt fairly with the Indians. He was also a friend of Walter's father. And what of Jacky Foster and Wiggy Wilson, who had kept Brant informed of activities at Cherry Valley?

Butler received the request with a laugh. "I never thought you would get soft-hearted, Joseph," he remarked. "You have the reputation of being the most blood-thirsty Indian in the Mohawk Valley. At Niagara they are talking about the way you massacred the helpless people at Wyoming in Pennsylvania."

"Me? At Wyoming?" cried Brant. "You know very well I wasn't there."

"The Whigs think you were. That is as good as the truth."

Brant saw through the game the Butlers were playing. They were massacring settlers and laying the blame at his door.

"I'll take credit for my achievements," he retorted, "but you and your father can keep your deeds for yourselves."

Walter Butler grinned.

"If you are in command, you can handle the Senecas tomorrow," Brant told Butler, "and God help the poor people of Cherry Valley."

"Are you getting sentimental, Joseph?" Butler taunted him. "I thought you believed that the only way to win the war was to wipe out the settlements. Prisoners are a nuisance, according to your own words."

It was difficult to swallow these words, for Brant had said them on several occasions. "Then you will not spare our friends?" he asked.

"The Senecas can hardly be expected to tell friend from foe."

The Seneca chiefs grunted their approval.

Joseph Brant knew when he was beaten. He could not risk losing the support of the Senecas. He stalked out of the council.

The morning of November 11, 1778 broke cold and stormy. Snow had fallen during the night. It gave way to sleet and rain at dawn. A low-hanging mist hid the fort and its cluster of houses. Brant, watching from the heights, sensed that Colonel Alden had been careless. The people had not been brought into the fort, for figures could be seen in the clearings.

Walter Butler waited for the mist to rise. It was high noon when he gave the order to advance. Six hundred and fifty Indians and Tories rushed down from the heights. A horseman fired at them. The shot was returned. The horseman, wounded, kept riding toward the fort.

The home of Robert Wells lay at the outskirts of the settlement. Brant liked Wells. The Whig was a square-shooter. Joseph wanted to have him spared. Butler had refused.

A plowed field lay between the Mohawk Chief and the Wells house. Brant, leaving his warriors, hastened across the broken soil. If he could get to the house ahead of the Senecas he might warn Wells and let him and his family escape. Halfway across the clearing he stopped. It was no use. The Senecas had beaten him to his objective.

A half-dressed officer left the Wells house and ran toward the fort, pursued by a yelling Seneca. The officer, middle-aged and portly, had no chance against the flying feet of the Indian. A tomahawk hurtled through the air. The officer fell on his face. The Seneca pounced upon him and tore away his scalp. Later, Brant learned that the victim was Colonel Ichabod Alden, the commandant of the fort.

He entered the Wells home, where blood-thirsty Senecas shrieked the scalp yell and dashed to and fro in search of plunder. Robert Wells knelt on the floor, his

scalpless head a mass of blood. He had been attacked
and killed while leading family devotions. Nearby lay his
wife and two children, also scalped. In the kitchen lay
the bodies of servants and two relatives.

A shriek drove Brant to the window. A Seneca was
dragging a young girl out of the woodpile. A Tory
rushed up to the Indian. He evidently was pleading with
the Seneca to spare the girl's life. The Seneca pushed
him aside roughly and buried his tomahawk in her head.
The whole Wells family, with the exception of a son who
was in school in Albany, was wiped out.

Cherry Valley became a mass of flames. Houses were
being set afire everywhere. Above the crackling of
timbers rose wails for mercy and the high-pitched yells
of the Senecas, who were now completely out of control. Butler and his Tories rushed the fort, only to be
beaten back by its defenders.

Joseph Brant got no thrill out of these events. Though
he was a full-blood Indian, this brutality which white
men had planned sickened him. His only desire was to
save as many Tories as possible. He met Little Aaron, a
Mohawk Chief who also had attended the Moor Charity
School. Little Aaron told Joseph that he had hidden Mr.
Dunlop, but that the Senecas had killed and scalped the
preacher's wife.

"Is this the civilization Dr. Wheelock used to preach?"
asked Little Arron, his lips turned down in disgust.

"The Butlers aren't civilized," retorted Brant.

The Senecas ignored the Tory attack on the fort. They
ran from house to house, dragged out helpless victims,
scalped and mutilated them. Brant made no attempt to
stop them. Walter Butler was in charge. Let him handle
the Senecas.

Smoke rose from the chimney of a log house. It clung
to the roof before blending with the heavy air. Brant
stared. How was it that this house had been overlooked?
He rushed across the clearing and entered the kitchen.

A strange sight met his eyes. A woman in a homespun

dress and apron was cooking at the fireplace. She seemed unaware of the horror that surrounded her.

"Woman," yelled Brant, "why don't you run for the fort or the woods? What are you doing here while your neighbors are being massacred?"

The woman raised a calm face. Her eyes held no fear. "I have nothing to worry about," she told the painted chief. "We are King's people."

Brant grasped her by the shoulder. "That excuse will get you nowhere today," he cried. "They have murdered the Wells family, who are as dear to me as your own."

The woman was still not convinced of her danger. "There is with the Indians one Joseph Brant," she said. "He will save us."

"I am Joseph Brant but I have not the command. I don't know as I can save you. But I'll do all that's in my power."

He looked out the window. Several Senecas were approaching the house. Tomahawks in their hands dripped blood. Scalps dangled at their belts.

Brant pushed the woman roughly toward a bunk at the side of the room. "Get into bed, quick," he ordered.

The woman obeyed. She pulled the covers up to her chin.

"Make believe you are sick," Brant advised her. "Senecas won't harm a sick woman. I'll hide the children." He tucked two small boys under the bed.

The Senecas came in, whooping, yelling. They encountered Captain Joseph Brant.

"There are no people here," he said defiantly, "except a sick woman. Go seek scalps elsewhere."

These orders did not please the Senecas. They debated the matter among themselves. Brant stood motionless before the bunk. His tomahawk was grasped firmly in his right hand. His determined look convinced the Senecas. They grunted and went out the door.

Brant ran to the end of the cabin and gave a shrill blast on his silver whistle. Several Mohawks answered the signal.

"Where is your paint?" Brant asked their leader.

With sure fingers, the Mohawk Chief placed the mark of his nation on the foreheads of the woman and her children. "You are probably safe," he told them, "but if a chance to escape offers itself, don't let it slip through your fingers."

The fort wasn't taken that day or the next. Rumor came through that reinforcements were coming from Schoharie and Fort Plain. Butler gathered his forces, the prisoners, the plunder. The whole party marched two miles away and camped for the night. Large fires were lighted. The warriors circled around the prisoners, whooping, threatening.

Disposition of the prisoners came up before a council. Brant asked that the women and children be allowed to return to Cherry Valley. Butler refused. A Seneca chief asked a question. Of what use were such helpless creatures on the long march back to Niagara? They voted with Brant, much to Butler's disgust. The women and children were released, except for two women who were taken to Niagara to exchange for Walter Butler's wife, who was in the hands of the Bostonians.

Lieutenant Colonel Stacey was the most prominent of the prisoners. Brant asked him where Bob McKean had been during the attack on Cherry Valley.

"Bob and his family pulled up stakes during the summer and moved over near Fort Plain," Stacey explained.

"He sent me a challenge once," said Brant. "I came to Cherry Valley to accept it. He is a fine soldier to run away like that."

"Captain McKean would not turn his back on an enemy where there was a chance of success," Stacey retorted.

"I know it. He is a brave man. I would have given more to take him than any other man in Cherry Valley and I would not have hurt one hair on his head."

Colonel John Butler received his son at Fort Niagara. Butler's conscience had troubled him since his attack upon Wyoming. The news that Cherry Valley had been wiped out by his son upset him. "I would have gone miles on my hands and knees to save the Wells family," he told Walter, "and why you did not do it, God only knows."

Molly Brant, who was living at Niagara, hated Lieutenant Colonel Stacey. She told Colonel Butler she had dreamed that she had Stacey's head and that she and the Indians were kicking it about. Butler sent her away with a gift of a painted keg of rum. The liquor did not stop Molly's dreams. The following night she and the Indians were again playing football with Stacey's head. Butler sent her another keg of rum and told her that Stacey would not be given up to her.

News came through of events which followed the Cherry Valley massacre. A runner told Brant that Wiggy Wilson had been visited by a party of soldiers and settlers, who demanded that the Tory tell the plans of his Indian friends. Wiggy couldn't tell them for the simple reason that he did not know. They produced a rope. In a few minutes Wiggy was swinging from a sour-apple tree. They let him struggle until he got blue in the face, thinking that such treatment might loosen his tongue or at least help his memory. The result was negative, so they cut him down. The experiment was repreated, this time at such length that it was some time before circulation could be rubbed back into his body. This frightened the settlers. They went home, leaving Wiggie the rope as a keepsake.

Brant listened to the story. At the close he commented dryly, "You may call me a savage, but I have never made war on women and children, nor have I hanged a neighbor on suspicion."

Chapter XXIV

"We Have You Outnumbered."

RUMORS filtered into Fort Niagara before the snow had left the hillsides. The Bostonians, angered by the attacks upon Wyoming and Cherry Valley, were sending a Great Blue Snake to crawl against the Senecas in the spring. General Sullivan was already gathering forces at Easton in Pennsylvania. He was preparing to cut his way through the wilderness to Tioga on the Susquehanna River. There he would be joined by General James Clinton and the New York regiments. The combined forces would sweep into the Finger Lake country to destroy the Seneca villages and thus cut off the granary of the British army.

Joseph Brant listened to the news, which was serious. In the rolling land of the Genesee Valley, crops grew in abundance; grain, vegetables, and fruit. Their loss would mean near starvation for the followers of the King. Something had to be done about it! But what? The invading army would be far superior to any force he and the Butlers could gather, in men, food and equipment. Brant had tried to win the Oneidas to his side during the winter. He had been unsuccessful, chiefly due to the efforts of Samuel Kirkland.

The first blow fell before the sun had burned the thongs of winter. A runner came in with the report that the Onondaga villages had been wiped out by a force from Fort Stanwix under Colonels Van Schaick and Willett. The Continentals had marched through snow and slush to attack the Onondagas, who had been caught

132

napping. All their houses had been destroyed. The
horses, pigs and other farm animals had been slaughtered.
The council fire of the Iroquois Confederacy had been
extinguished.

Early June found the Mohawk River filled with batteaux from Schenectady to Canajoharie, from which
point they would be transported overland to Lake Glimmerglass and then floated down a creek to the Susquehanna.

Joseph Brant, watching from the heights above his
former home, could see the clumsy boats landing on the
flats near Canajoharie. Tents dotted the landscape, hundreds of tents, around which swarmed thousands of
brightly-uniformed soldiers. Brant recognized the gray
and green of the Third New Yorkers. The Mohawk Chief
held this regiment in respect, for he had seen its defense of
Fort Stanwix. He also knew the reputation of those
brown and buff Pennsylvania troops who were drilling on
the flats. The odds were against him. It would be useless
to attack these regiments with his handful of Indians and
Tories. He would watch their movements, raid their
camps occasionally, or pick off isolated scouts.

The batteaux moved southward across the hills on
wagons and sleds. The Pennsylvanians were guarding the
convoy. These riflemen were excellent shots. The Indians
kept their distance, but made their presence known
through blood-curdling whoops and an occasional gun-
shot which caused little damage. The batteaux were
rowed down Glimmerglass without accident. Clinton's
army camped at the foot of the lake. There was much
parading, shouting and speech-making.

Brant learned that the Continentals, while awaiting
orders from General Sullivan, were celebrating the third
anniversary of their Declaration of Independence. That
night he and his Indians added to the excitement by
circling the camp. From the safety of the forest, they let
out wierd whoops which made the Continentals sleep
with their clothes on.

Joseph Brant did not tarry at Glimmerglass. What could a handful of Indians and Tories do against two thousand Continentals? The Senecas had stayed home to defend their villages. So had the Cayugas. Only the faithful Mohawks were following Joseph.

The Chief counted heads. His command consisted of sixty Indians and twenty Tories. It was discouraging, very discouraging. He who had been the leader of the Six Nations was losing his grip to Red Jacket, that talkative squaw man. A lesser man might have given up the cause, but Brant did not know how to quit.

A runner brought the news that Count Pulaski and his cavalry, who had been protecting the settlements west of the Hudson River, had ridden away from Minisink. A raid in that direction would be of more value than bothering Clinton's army.

Brant's small force crossed the two branches of the Delaware River. In a few days they were within thirty miles of the fortifications of West Point. They halted a mile from Minisink. With Brant were some of the most rabid Tories. These men stripped off their uniforms and painted their bodies red and black in the Mohawk manner. They boasted openly of cruelties.

As Joseph Brant listened to the laughter of the Pale Faces and the grunts of the Mohawks, he turned over in his mind thoughts which had troubled him ever since the war began. The white man, given a farm and a family, would live in peace and labor mightily to advance civilization. But let hatred once enter his soul, he was worse than the Indian. He would commit murder against his own neighbors. He would make war on women and children. Brant liked to fight. He had killed men and had scalped them. But he would not stoop to lift the scalp of a woman or a child.

The attack upon Minisink came at dead of night. Several houses rose in flames before the inhabitants knew what was happening. Even the stockaded fort and the mill were set afire before the Indians retired to the forest with prisoners and plunder. In the morning they started for the Delaware River.

Colonel Hathorn, in command at Minisink, gathered a force of one hundred and fifty militiamen and set out in pursuit. From the heights, he saw Brant's party preparing to ford the river where it was joined by the Lackawaxen. He decided to head off the Indians and Tories.

Brant's scouts learned of Hathorn's plans. It was easy to ambush the militiamen, who had lost sight of the Indians in the descent from the hills to the river. Brant wheeled to the rear of Hathorn, catching him and his men in a narrow ravine.

The Mohawk Chief decided to outbluff Hathorn, who outnumbered him two to one. He stepped from the undergrowth and signalled. "We have you outnumbered," he cried. "We have you surrounded. We can easily overpower and destroy you. I ask you to surrender before blood has been shed. If you refuse, I cannot answer for the consequences."

Hathorn hesitated, for he saw that the situation was desperate, even hopeless.

A hot-headed militiaman answered for the colonel. Raising his gun to his shoulder, he fired at Joseph Brant. The Mohawk Chief vanished into the bushes, fingering angrily the place where the bullet had torn away part of his belt. Another inch and he would have been a dead Indian.

The militiamen rushed forward. They broke order as they splashed through the shallow waters of the creek. Before they could form on the other side, Brant let out a war whoop. He ran toward the creek, tomahawk in hand, followed by red and "white" Indians. The militiamen, surrounded and confused, were easy victims. The naked savages and their blood-thirsty allies swooped down on them, shooting, tomahawking, knifing.

Joseph Brant fought in blind anger. He had liked that belt. Sir William had given it to him. Now it was useless. He wielded his tomahawk mightily. It was red with the blood of Pale Faces. His frayed belt contained several fresh scalps.

He heard a groan from the thicket. Pushing aside the bushes, he came upon a colonel, mortally wounded. Should he leave this man to lie there and be eaten by wolves or should he kill him?

The officer spoke faintly. "Water," he gasped.

Brant's lips curled. His first thought was to let the fellow die of thirst. His better side triumphed. Scooping up a handful of water from a brooklet, he pressed it to the man's lips.

"Thank you," said the colonel. "It was kind of you, Captain Brant."

The Mohawk Chief moved behind the colonel. He would not leave this brave fellow for the wolves to chew while he was still alive. He engaged the colonel in conversation. The officer talked of his home and his family. His mind was not upon death. Brant's tomahawk descended. The colonel's days were over. His scalp decorated the belt of a Mohawk chief.

Brant did not tarry. He hated himself for his weakness. But was it weakness, he argued with himself? Was it better to kill a man or leave him a victim of the animals of the forest?

He remained in this mood when another officer rushed up to him. This man's coat was torn from his body. His face was scratched by brambles. The officer halted. He gave the sign of the Masonic Order.

"Who are you?" asked Brant, lowering his tomahawk.

"Major Wood. I thank you, Brother," The man's eyes were shifty. Brant took a dislike to him immediately. But if the officer were a Mason, he would be spared. Masons did not murder their brothers in cold blood. Brant took Wood prisoner.

Sundown brought an end to the struggle. The ravine was filled with the scalped and stripped bodies of militiamen. Out of one hundred and fifty who had given battle, only thirty were not dead or captured. The Indians

rejoiced at camp that night. They had lost few men. So
they danced around the fires with the painted Tories,
rejoicing in the scalps and plunder they had taken. They
poked fun at the captives and tortured them in a manner
enjoyable to Indians.

Major Wood kept close to Joseph Brant, his face
white, his whole body trembling. Brant, watching the
cowering officer, fought off a desire to give him to the
Indians.

Night came and with it sleep. Wood had no equipment. His body was almost naked. Brant came to him
with a gaudy blanket.

"Lie on this," he said shortly. He ordered Wood to be
tied to two Indians.

Wood protested loudly. "I am a gentleman," he cried.
"I'll lie between the Indians. I won't try to escape. I
won't even move during the night."

"On your honor as a Mason?"

"On my honor as a Mason."

Wood could not sleep. The horrors of the day danced
before his eyes. Friends, neighbors and relatives had been
slaughtered in the ravine while he had escaped through a
lie. He was no Mason, though he had learned their sign.
It was surprising that Brant had taken him at his word.
What if the Mohawk Chief learned the truth? Wood lay
there, listening to the snores of the Indians. He might
make a dash for liberty. But no, he had given his word. He
would keep it.

Dawn approached. The fire had burned low. Wood was
lying close to the embers. He smelled smoke. Looking
down, he saw that the edge of the blanket upon which
he was lying was afire. The Indians beside him were
snoring loudly. Should he try to put out the fire? If he
did, he felt sure that some watching Indian would knock
him over the head. So he lay quietly, hoping that the
fire would go out.

Joseph Brant, sleeping nearby, also smelled smoke.
Rising to his feet, he stamped out the fire. In the dim

light, Wood could not make out the Indian's features,
but he recognized the angry voice which cried, "Damn
you, you have ruined my best blanket."

Wood lay shivering in the dawn. The Mohawk Chief
had gone back to his place. Wood was thinking. What a
man this Brant was! What other redskin would have
given his best blanket to a prisoner he could have killed
outright?

Brant and his party hurried toward the Mohawk Val-
ley. They fell on an isolated settlement and took a few
prisoners. It was an unfortunate adventure for the
Mohawk Chief, for he received a wound in his big toe.
Limping badly, he led his forces west to join Colonel
Butler, who was gathering the Senecas in an effort to
bother Sullivan's army. The prisoners were sent to
Niagara. It was the last Brant saw of Major Wood.

Together with Butler, he prepared a barricade at Newtown. They hoped to trap Sullivan's large force before it
could get under way. The Tories and Indians fought
bravely until Sullivan's artillery came into action.
Nothing could make redskins stand up before cannon.
The sound frightened them. The impact drove them
away. The struggle at Newtown was brief but bloody.
Even the Indian women fought behind the barricade.
Butler and Brant retreated to Catharine's Town, leaving
their dead on the field of battle. The way to the Seneca
villages lay open.

The Indians were defeated, dissatisfied. The Senecas,
in particular, could not take setbacks. Red Jacket had
gone with the expedition against Sullivan. Though he was
twenty-nine years old, it was the first time he had ever
been on the warpath. Due to his fleetness of foot, he
had been employed as a messenger and much of his
running had been in a direction away from the enemy.

Cornplanter came to Brant in anger. The half-breed
was unwilling to leave the Seneca country open to the
Great Blue Snake. He could not understand Butler's
indifference. He was disgusted with Red Jacket.

"I will tell you about that little coward," said Cornplanter to Brant. "Do you know where he was during the battle?"

"I didn't see him behind the barricade."

"Why wasn't he there? Because he stayed behind in camp to cut up a cow." Cornplanter's lips turned down in scorn.

"What!"

"I have the facts. I have a new name for him, too. I call him Cow Killer."

Brant grunted. He liked the name. It fitted Red Jacket better than the red coat the Seneca wore.

Washington's orders to General Sullivan were clear. Sullivan was to destroy the Indian settlements. The New Hampshire general obeyed his orders to the letter. Houses were burned. Apple trees were girdled. Vegetable crops were destroyed or taken. The Blue Snake that was the Continental Army marched up the shore of Seneca Lake, laying waste to the countryside. It met with little resistance until it approached the great Seneca castle.

Here Brant and Cornplanter decided to make a stand. Red Jacket was opposed. He began to retreat.

Cornplanter stepped in front of the orator. His long, lean body trembled with anger. "Stop, Cow Killer!" he cried.

Red Jacket was small and wiry. Sharp eyes shone bright beneath a towering forehead. Beside him stood his wife, a quiet woman.

"It is no use to fight," retorted Red Jacket. "I hate the Pale Face more than you do. After all, you are part Pale Face."

Cornplanter took a step forward. He did not like to be reminded of his mixed blood.

The woman stepped between them.

Cornplanter's hand dropped from his knife. He laughed aloud.

Red Jacket had nothing to say. He could argue with Cornplanter. What did the half-breed know of the

thoughts of a pure-blooded Seneca? Cornplanter was half
Pale Face. He did not feel the deep hatred for white
civilization, education and Christianity that burned in
Red Jacket's breast.

"Run away, Cow Killer!" yelled Cornplanter. "Your
tongue is your war club." Turning to the woman he said,
"Leave that man, for he is a coward."

Brant and Cornplanter waited near the Seneca Castle
for the Blue Snake, which was crawling slowly forward.
For days scouts had reported that the Pale Face soldiers
had been filling their stomachs with wild grapes and
apples from the Seneca orchards.

Among Sullivan's officers was Thomas Boyd, a scout
noted for his daring. Boyd and a party of twenty-seven
men roamed the forest in advance of the Blue Snake.
They fell into an ambush. All but eleven were killed or
captured. Among the prisoners was Thomas Boyd.

The scout was brought before Captain Brant, who
liked this fearless and defiant fellow. When Boyd gave
the sign of the Masonic Order, Joseph decided to save
the scout, though he was getting sick and tired of sparing
Masons. He sent Boyd and the other captives to Colonel
Butler with orders to spare them.

That night Brant returned to the Seneca castle. Bright
fires were burning. Senecas whooped and danced around
a group of victims. The ceremony was almost over. A
sergeant lay dead on the ground. His body had been
horribly mutilated. The Senecas were torturing Boyd.

Brant felt sick. There was nothing he could do for
Boyd now. He left the scene and sought Colonel Butler.

"What is the meaning of this?" he yelled.

Butler spread his hands helplessly. "I couldn't do a
thing to stop them, Joseph," he said. "But I couldn't
watch it."

Brant turned on his heel. As he passed the fire, he saw
a Seneca dancing around with the head of Boyd stuck on
a spear.

The Blue Snake reached the Seneca castle two days

later. The Indians had vanished. The bodies of Boyd and his companions were buried beneath a wild plum tree. The Continentals took revenge on the settlement. Everything was destroyed.

Chapter XXV

"It Tastes Much Better than Strawberries."

BEFORE the Hunter's Moon had waned, the snow goose hovered over Niagara and dropped a generous supply of feathers on the fort and the bark houses which sheltered the remains of the once powerful Iroquois nations. The hand of Go-ho-ne, the Winter, grasped the waters of lake and stream. And night after night the panther that was the North Wind howled as he piled the snow against the ramparts and blew his cold breath through the walls of the bark houses.

Joseph Brant had no reason for leaving the fort. Susanna had died some years before. The Mohawk Chief took a third wife, Catharine, the daughter of a Mohawk sachem of the Tortoise clan. Into their bark house came Isaac and Christina, children of Brant's first marriage.

Isaac at fourteen was a shifty-eyed boy with a quick temper. He had lived at Fort Niagara since early in the war. Much of his time had been spent with the soldiers, from whom he had picked up some English and a fondness for imitating all that was bad. He swore like a trooper. He also was known to be light-fingered. Only recently he had been flogged publicly for stealing from members of the garrison.

Captain Brant took his son in hand. They hunted together in fair weather and foul. Isaac listened half-heartedly to the legends of the Mohawks and found them tame compared to the yarns he had heard at the fort. Brant soon discovered that his son cared not a thing for the traditions of the Mohawks. And over him crept a wave of bitterness directed not only at Isaac but at the Pale Faces who had influenced the boy.

Cold and hunger did not improve Brant's disposition. And the sufferings of his people cut him to the heart. He had led them into the war. He had told them that the Great White Father over the Great Lake would protect them from the Bostonians.

And what had been the result of this loyalty? Whole villages had been destroyed by the Great Blue Snake. Warriors lay unburied far from their homes, while their spirits wandered around in a state of great unhappiness. If Brant had not listened to the British, the Seneca orchards might not have been girdled. The Iroquois might have learned to live at peace with the Bostonians. But no; as King Hendrick often had said, "The Pale Face is like a worm that cuts off the corn as soon as it appears."

Joseph arrived at the same conclusion he had reached the night before the Battle of Oriskany. The Pale Face was forever protecting something and it was always the Pale Face who was being protected. The poor Indian did not enter into his plans. Maybe that was what Sir William had meant when he had said, "Joseph, take care of your people."

The war would end some day. Either the King or the Bostonians would win. What would happen to the Iroquois? The Bostonians would take away their lands. That was sure. Brant had cast his lot and the fortunes of his people with the King. What would the King do for the Indians if he won? Brant decided he would no longer consider the interests of the Pale Face but would devote his time and energy toward protecting the Six Nations.

With this thought in mind, he went among the Senecas, the Cayugas, the Onondagas and the Mohawks. He roused them from the stupor caused by their defeat and by the oratory of Red Jacket. An expedition of Indians left Niagara while snow still covered the ground. Oneida Castle was totally destroyed. Thus did the Iroquois punish the nation which had broken the chain of the Confederacy.

Brant did not stop here. He moved on to attack the Schoharie forts. Sap was running from the maples as he and his band of fifty Indians passed the ruins of Cherry Valley. Scouts ran ahead of the main party, their footsteps soft as the tread of a panther. Harpersfield was burned and plundered.

The generous snow goose followed Brant from Niagara. She dropped her blessings in the form of large, wet feathers which clung to his hunting costume and made his moccasins heavy as lead. He called a halt.

"We shall wait here until the snow goose goes home," he told his followers.

Nearly three feet of snow fell during the night. It weighed down the sapling shelters the Indians had thrown up. It filled the trails with a soft whiteness that made travel difficult. Brant sent out scouts. They returned in midmorning with the news that a small party of Pale Faces was working in a sugar bush about five miles toward the east.

Brant ordered an advance. The Indians grumbled because their snow moccasins had been left behind at Niagara but they obeyed their leader. Smoke was rising from a maple grove straight ahead. The Indians formed a circle which closed in on the sap-gatherers. Brant could see about a dozen men standing around fires over which kettles had been hung. Smaller containers caught the sap from maple trees in the grove. The men, unconscious of danger, were laughing and talking together.

Three men fell at Brant's order to fire. The others either dropped on their stomachs or dove into the lean-tos near the fire. The surprise had been complete.

"You are in my power," called Brant from behind a tree. He did not trust the Pale Faces.

A white man stepped out into the open. It was Captain Alexander Harper of Schoharie.

Brant rushed up to him with tomahawk uplifted.

Recognizing Harper, he said, "Harper, I am sorry to find you here."

"Why are you sorry, Captain Brant?" Harper's question showed his fearlessness.

"Because I must kill you, though we were in school together." Brant's arm fell to his side. Why should he kill this man? Harper might have information that was of value. Looking the white man in the eye he asked, "Are there any regular troops at the Schoharie forts?"

Harper hesitated. If he told the truth, he would have to admit there were none. So he lied. "Why yes, Joseph, three hundred trained troops came in a couple of days ago."

It was impossible for Brant to conceal his surprise at this news. Leaving Harper standing there, he went into conference with two chiefs, to whom he told Harper's news.

"Is he telling the truth?" asked one chief. "The bite of a forked tongue is like the sting of bad arrows."

"I've never known him to lie."

"Fifty Indians are not enough," said the second chief.

Harper and ten other prisoners were bound hand and foot and placed in one of the leantos. The Indians argued with Brant that the men should be killed and scalped but he overruled them. These Pale Faces might give up information.

Brant questioned Harper again the next morning. The man from Schoharie stuck to his story. So the Indians and their prisoners plodded west through the snow toward Niagara. The booty from Harpersfield was strapped to the shoulders of the prisoners. One old man was unable to keep up the pace. Brant called to him an Indian whose body was painted black. This man of death dropped back with the prisoner. Soon he reappeared with a scalp dangling from his belt.

At Oquage the party constructed rude boats and floated down the flood waters of the Susquehanna to its junction with the Chemung. Here Captain Brant was taken with fever and the party could travel only on alternate days.

Brant cured his illness with an Indian remedy. One sunny afternoon he had two warriors help him to a rocky cliff overlooking the river. Here he watched until a rattlesnake came out to sun itself on the rocks. After cutting a strong stick from a nearby tree and fashioning one end into a fork, he crawled toward the snake, which showed its displeasure by making sounds like dice rattling in a gourd. The Mohawk Chief smiled to himself. Here he was, the primitive savage, trying to kill a snake with an outworn weapon when a rifle hung from his shoulder. He took aim and pulled the trigger. His two companions rushed up to where the headless rattler lay writhing.

"Take him back to camp and make me some rattlesnake soup," said Brant. "That will drive the evil spirits out of me."

Brant ate of the soup, saying, "It tastes much better than strawberries."

And his followers knew that their leader had been near death, for strawberries grew along the path to the Happy Hunting Ground.

Provisions ran out. Meals consisted of a handful of corn per man. The Indians found the carcass of a horse left the preceding summer by the Great Blue Snake. Wolves had devoured most of the meat. The Indians made soup of the bones and ate ravenously of it. They met a Seneca straggling back to his village after wintering in Niagara. He was leading a horse. Brant debated with himself. Should the Seneca be allowed to keep his animal for spring planting? Or should his own men be fed? The horse was killed and the Indians had their first square meal in days.

Chapter XXVI

"We Are between Two Hells."

THE Mohawk Chief did not rest long at Niagara. The Strawberry Moon was in its first quarter when he swooped down on the Mohawk Valley. Scouts had told him that Colonel Peter Gansevoort was using the militia to protect supplies being sent up the river to Fort Stanwix. Brant made a feint at this convoy and then hurried behind it to ruin crops and burn homesteads along the south side of the river as far as Fort Plain.

The big invasion of the Mohawk Valley came in the autumn. Sir John Johnson, the Johnny of Joseph's boyhood, with British regulars and Butler's Rangers, met Brant and his Indians in the Susquehanna Valley. The party swept up the Schoharie Valley, burned houses, rustled cattle, and pounded at the forts with mortars which the Indians called "grasshoppers". The forts refused to surrender, so the invaders hurried on toward the Mohawk. They reached the river at Fort Hunter. Here news came that General Robert Van Rensselaer and a large force of militia and Continentals were marching toward them from Albany.

Johnson and Brant retreated toward the west. At Stone Arabia they were held up by the fierce resistance of a small party of militia. After these defenders had been crushed and scalped, the invading party divided, Brant and the Indians crossing the Mohawk. Settlers fled in terror before the advancing armies on both sides of the river.

With the Indians was Cornplanter, that son of a white

147

trader and a Seneca woman. He and Brant were together much of the time. Cornplanter was not proud of his mixed blood.

"When I was a child," he told the Mohawk Chief, "I played with the butterfly, the grasshopper and the frogs. As I grew up, I began to play with the Indian boys and they took notice of my skin being a different color than theirs and spoke of it. I asked my mother and she told me my father was a resident of Albany. I ate my victuals out of a dish. I grew up to be a young man and married me a wife but I had no kettle or gun.

"I then knew where my father lived and went to see him and found he was a white man and spoke the Pale Face language. He gave victuals while I was at his house, but when I started home he gave me neither provision to eat on the way nor a kettle or a gun. Neither did he tell me that the Bostonians were about to rebel against the King."

"It is the way of the Pale Face," said Brant, remembering some of the promises which had been made to him.

"The different kinds the Great Spirit made separate," Cornplanter commented, "and not to mix with and disturb each other. But the Pale Face has broken this command by mixing his color with the Indians. The Indians have done better by not doing so."

Captain Brant had nothing to say. Many times had he heard rumors that he was partly white. That he knew was not true, but the rumors upset him just the same. He was relieved when a young Mohawk interrupted the conversation. The warrior carried a white child in his arms. He explained that a Tory had taken the baby at Fort Hunter.

Brant frowned. "Take the child back to the fort," he told the young warrior. On a piece of bark he wrote, "Sir: I send you by one of my runners a child which he will deliver that you may know that whatever others do, I do not make war upon women and children. I am sorry to say that I have those engaged with me in the service who are more savage than the savages themselves." He signed with a flourish, "Joseph Thayendanegea."

Van Rensselaer followed closely on the heels of the invaders. Tired and desperate, Brant and his Indians hurried past Fort Herkimer, dragging with them plunder and prisoners. The Mohawk Chief limped badly, for he had been shot in the heel at Stone Arabia.

Cornplanter had taken as prisoner one John Abeel, a trader well known in the Mohawk Valley. The Seneca chief brought this man before Captain Brant.

"My name is John Abeel," Cornplanter said, addressing the trader. "I am known to my people as Cornplanter. I am your son! You are my father! You are now my prisoner and subject to the customs of Indian warfare. But you shall not be harmed. You need not fear. I am a warrior! Many are the scalps I have taken. Many prisoners have I tortured to death. I am your son! I am a warrior! I was anxious to see you and to greet you in friendship. I went to your cabin and took you by force. But your life will be spared. Indians love their friends and their kindred and treat them with kindness.

"If you now choose to follow the fortunes of your son and live with our people, I will cherish your old age with plenty of venison and you shall live easy. But if it is your choice to return to your fields and live with your white children, I will send a party of my trusty young men to conduct you back to safety.

"I respect you, my father. You have been friendly to the Indians. They are your friends."

John Abeel made his choice. He was sent back to the Mohawk Valley.

Joseph Brant took part in no more mass raids on the Mohawk Valley. It became clear to him that the war was drawing to a close and that the British would be the losers. So he went to talk with the Western Indians at Sandusky in the Ohio country. While there he was wounded in the leg accidentally with his own knife. He returned to Detroit, where he spent the winter and part of the next year. News came through to him that a raiding party from Oswego under Major Ross and Walter Butler had been defeated by Colonel Marinus Willett and the Bostonians at Johnstown. In the retreat toward Canada, Walter Butler had been killed and scalped.

Joseph Brant was still full of fight. On Christmas Day, 1782, he wrote to Sir John Johnson:

"We are between two hells. I am sure you will assist all you can to let us have an expedition early in the spring, let it be a great or small one. Let us not hang our heads between our knees and be looking there. I beg of you, don't tell us to go hunt deer and find ourselves shoes because we shall soon forget the war, for we are gone too far that way already against the rebels to be doing other things . . . . I am as much forward to go to war as I ever did but I am not so well contented as I used to be formerly, because the warriors are in want. They are treated worse instead of better."

It was too late. The peacemakers were already in Paris preparing the final treaty.

The Iroquois bowstring had been broken. Their council fires had been put out by the blood of their own people. The Great Spirit had spoken to the whirlwind and it was still. And the red man's sun had been darkened, for the Great Spirit had drawn his sable garment before its shining face and left his red children to roam in gloom and uncertainty.

Chapter XXVII

"A Little Bird Came to Me Yesterday."

THE British still held Fort Niagara in defiance of the victorious Americans. The three thousand Indians camped there were becoming a problem for Colonel Maclean, the commandant of the fort. With the close of the war, the government in Quebec had lost all interest in the Iroquois. Sometimes it seemed to Maclean that Governor Haldimand had washed his hands of the entire matter. It was certainly true that supplies for the Indians were coming in smaller quantities each month.

Maclean also felt concerned about the attitude of one Captain Joseph Brant. The Mohawk Chief knew too much for an Indian. He wanted answers to questions and insisted that Maclean supply them. It was impossible to dodge the man.

Maclean was in the midst of a long letter to Governor Haldimand when Captain Brant was announced. Maclean opened his mouth to tell the orderly he was busy. He looked up to find Brant standing before him.

The Mohawk Chief threw aside his blue blanket bordered with red. He wore beneath it a short green coat with silver epaulets. His blue leggins and his moccasins were trimmed with white beads. Around his throat hung a necklace with a pendant in the form of a crescent. His headdress consisted of three drooping feathers.

Maclean's eyes caught these details, also the tomahawk with "J. Thayendanegea" engraved on the handle. "Good day, Captain Brant," he said, forcing a smile to his lips.

Brant's slight nod of recognition did not disturb a

single feather of his headdress. For a long moment he stared at Maclean, his eyes narrowed, his lips curling at the corners. "I came to inquire as to why my people are being given a picnic today."

Maclean squirmed. How did this fellow know that an American representative was due at Niagara to give official announcement of the terms of peace? How did Brant learn that the Indians were being sent away for the day so they would not meet the American? Surely there had been no leak from Maclean's office.

"Do you object to our being kind to your people?" asked the British officer.

"Your kindness could be practiced here and not five miles away, Colonel Maclean."

"The orders came from higher up," Maclean admitted.

"And good soldiers always obey orders?" Brant's sarcasm was withering.

Maclean flushed. He was familiar with Brant's attitude toward military discipline. Hadn't the Mohawk Chief once told him that the Indians were free as the air they breathed, that he would take orders from no man? How could a British officer be expected to understand such a person?

"And why must my people be entertained with kegs of fire water?" asked Brant.

"A gift from Colonel Butler."

Brant's face darkened like a thundercloud. Maclean wished he had kept this information to himself.

"The little birds are often kind to the poor Indian," Brant said. "A little bird came to me yesterday and told me that the representative of the Bostonians will be here today. Evidently you did not wish for him to see the poor Indian in his present condition. The Bostonians knew the Indian when he was free, when he hunted and fished in the country which the Great Spirit had given to him. I agree that the Bostonian might be shocked at sight of the poor Indians here. But one poor Indian is not going on your picnic, Colonel Maclean. Good day."

Maclean watched him leave the room. Poor Indian, had Brant said? Surely there was one Indian who could not be placed in that class. Maclean's quill flew along the paper.

"Captain Brant," he wrote to Haldimand, "though a brave fellow who has been a faithful, active subject of the King, has been most troublesome, because he is better instructed and much more intelligent than any other Indian.

"He is strongly attached to the interest of his countrymen, for which I do honor him, but he would be so much more sensible of the miserable situation in which we have left this unfortunate people, that I do believe he would do a great deal of mischief here at this time."

Captain Brant met the messenger from the United States of America. From him he learned that no provision had been made for the Indians in the treaty, but that the State of New York and the Provincial Congress were both ready and willing to talk with Brant and the Iroquois at a time and place which the Indians might choose.

The Indians returned from the picnic riotously drunk. One of them, a Delaware, fell head foremost into a kettle of boiling soup and was burned so badly that he died two days later. Others were for taking the warpath immediately against settlers whose land hunger was causing them to move into the Seneca country. Brant vetoed their plans, but he also decided to wait before holding a council to get their opinions about a time and a place for the treaty.

John Deseronto had long been one of Brant's best friends. They both had lived in the Mohawk Valley. They had gone to England together at the beginning of the war and had made the dangerous journey from New York to Oquage. Deseronto had been a faithful warrior. Many times had he and Brant fought side by side. So the two Mohawks travelled to Quebec to see Governor Haldimand, who received them graciously.

"The Six Nations and their allies have heard that the King their Father has made peace with his children the Bostonians," Brant said to Haldimand, "and when they heard it, they found that they were forgot and no mention was made of them in said peace, so they have sent me to ask whether it is true that they are not partakers of that peace with the King and the Bostonians."

"That is true," Haldimand admitted.

"But why?" asked John Deseronto.

"I don't know. I had nothing to do with making the treaty. That was made in Paris in France."

John Deseronto argued the matter in his broken English until Haldimand's face turned red as a beet.

"It is no use to talk that way, John," said Brant. "If our people are not part of the treaty, we must make one of our own with the Bostonians."

Deseronto grunted.

"But we won't get much satisfaction there," Brant added, turning to Haldimand. "We Mohawks will not be able to keep our land, for we lived in the country the Bostonians want most. We cannot go back. And we have nowhere to go, unless you deed us some land on British soil."

Haldimand knew Brant was right. He also had read Maclean's letter. So he asked, "Where would you wish to locate?"

"The Bay of Quinte," was Deseronto's prompt answer.

"I think that could be arranged. Would you move all of the Mohawks there?"

Deseronto nodded.

"And you, Captain Brant?"

In his mind, Brant was turning over the possibilities of all the Mohawks living together. He and Deseronto were both leaders. They would not wish to take orders from each other.

"No," he answered. "I think it better if John goes to the Bay of Quinte with the people of the Lower Castle at Fort Hunter and I choose another site for the Mohawks of the Upper Castle at Canajoharie."

Haldimand accepted Deseronto's silence as agreement. "Very well," he said, "there is a fine tract on the Grand River which flows into Lake Erie farther to the west. Would you care to go there, Captain Brant?"

"I shall think the matter over."

Brant and Deseronto returned to Niagara and told the Iroquois of their plans. The Mohawks were enthusiastic about the proposals. The Senecas, who had offered the Mohawks part of their own lands, were highly insulted. The Western Indians also stood opposed. So Brant decided to postpone any answer to Haldimand which might upset the delicate relations now existing between him and the other Indian nations.

The preliminary treaty with the United States of America was held at Fort Stanwix late in the summer of 1784. Joseph Brant, Cornplanter and Red Jacket were the leading representatives of the Six Nations.

Attempts at a settlement were blocked by misunderstandings. The Pale Faces did not know whether Brant and the other chiefs were speaking for all the Indians or for the Iroquois alone. The Indians were not sure whether they were talking with representatives of the State of New York or of the thirteen colonies.

Governor Clinton of New York addressed the Indians. He reminded them that they had fought against his government during the war. He asked them what points they wished to have arranged before they met with the representatives of the thirteen colonies later in the year.

Brant's reply was brief. "You warned us not to be led astray by evil-minded persons," he said. "We thank you for this advice. We take it for granted that you know we are exposed to deception, otherwise you would not have warned us. This we shall observe. We shall be on our guard and we suppose it is necessary, as our lands will be an object of jealousy.

"We would first meet commissioners of the whole

thirteen states and after that if any matters should remain between us and any particular state, that we should then attend to them. At the same time we are fully determined notwithstanding all this to make a final settlement with you and do all we can for that purpose."

Clinton asked for the cession of Indian lands. Brant and Cornplanter agreed that they would give up some territory. The Iroquois would not dispose of any land within the State of New York without the latter's consent. The final treaty would be made late in the autumn at Fort Stanwix.

Brant did not wait for this treaty-making. Instead, he continued negotiations with Governor Haldimand. A tract of land one hundred miles long was granted to him in the name of the Crown. According to the deed, this land was "upon the banks of the river Ouise, commonly called the Grand River, running into Lake Erie, of six miles breadth on each side of the river beginning at Lake Erie, and extending in that proportion to the head of said river; which the Mohawks, and others of the Six Nations who had either lost their possessions in the war, or wished to retire from them to the British, with their posterity, were to enjoy forever."

News of the treaty of Fort Stanwix reached Brant early in the following spring. Red Jacket had been opposed to burying the hatchet. He had spoken with great eloquence. Cornplanter, on the other hand, had seen the folly of war with the United States. He had advised against risking the loss of all the Indian lands. The treaty provisions practically drove the Iroquois out of New York. Red Jacket, dissatisfied, went home to stir up the Senecas against Cornplanter.

Brant was angry, not at the treaty or the chiefs who made it, for he could not have done better; but the United States had held as hostage, among others, Captain Aaron Hill, his son-in-law and personal representative at the treaty-making.

Brant aired his feelings in a letter to James Monroe, an

assemblyman from Virginia whom he had met at Niagara. "We mean to go through with it and be done with it," he wrote, referring to the treaty, "that every body should mind their own business and be happy. This is our customs and manners of the Mohawks, whenever engaged in any thing. They are always active and true; no double faces at war or any other business . . . . These low live tricks confuse us very much. I believe we shall be at last prevented of becoming friends with you. If it should be so, the fault shall not be ours, which I hope you shall find so. If I could see you, I could explain better than in a letter half English and half Indian. But I am unwilling to go to a conference while my friends are detained."

Despite this protest, Hill was held for six months, or until the Mohawks returned certain white prisoners.

Brant went to England in 1785. He talked with such prominent men as Fox, Sheridan, Burke, Lord Sidney and the Prince of Wales.

The theme of his argument was as follows:

The Mohawks had long been friends of the King. They had often fought and had freely bled for the British cause. All they wanted was to have their claims attended to so they could stock their farms and get clothing and other necessities. Were the Mohawks still considered Britain's allies? If so, it was hard to believe that such firm friends and allies could be so neglected by a nation remarkable for its honor and glory, a nation whom the Mohawks had served with so much zeal and finality.

And the answer was always the same:

No country, however rich, could make good the losses of individuals suffered in a contest which had taken an unfavorable turn. The King could not consent to the demands of the Mohawks. He would recommend that they continue united in councils and that they conduct their measures with temper and moderation.

Joseph also made claims for half pay as Captain. When the claims were refused, he replied with a characteristic lack of self-interest, "When I joined the English at the beginning of the war, it was purely on account of my forefathers' engagements with the King. I always looked upon these engagements or covenants between the King and the Indian Nations as a sacred thing. I received pay during the war. If the King doesn't see the way clear to grant me a pension, I beg of him to think no more of it. If I was to get it and there were doubts about the propriety of it, I should not be happy. I think it best to go without it."

Brant's trip to England brought one reward. At Fort Hunter, prior to the war, he had translated the Book of Mark from the New Testament into Mohawk. The manuscript had been worked on during the winters at Niagara. It was now printed in a new edition of the English Book of Prayer for the Mohawk nation which Daniel Claus edited.

The preface read, "This is the first of the Gospels which has appeared *intire* in that language (Mohawk); and it will be a valuable acquisition to the Indians, who may hereby gain a more perfect knowledge of our blessed Saviour's doctrine and miracles, and of the way to salvation through his meritorious death and sufferings. It will probably be the more acceptable to the Indians for being translated by a person who is of their own nation and kindred. A version of some other parts of the New Testament may soon be expected from Captain BRANT; and he deserves great consideration for thus employing his time and talents to promote the honour of God, and spiritual welfare of his brethren."

Chapter XXVIII

"We Can Retreat No Further."

JOSEPH Brant returned to America to find Pale Face settlers spreading across New York and Pennsylvania into that section which lay between Lake Erie and the Ohio River. The Western Indians, thrown into a panic, were attacking the whites at every opportunity. The older chiefs wanted peace but they could not hold the young warriors in check.

Brant's attitude at this time of crisis caused confusion among both the Americans and the British. He talked of peace and evidently encouraged the British to act as mediators between the new government of the United States and the Western Indians. He went to Miami and sat in council with the tribes from the Ohio River country, but he said nothing about any results he may have arrived at there.

The American government, being inexperienced and somewhat cocky after its victory over the British, decided that it would put an end to all this foolishness. Accordingly, General St. Clair and a large body of militia marched into the Miami country to wipe out every redskin in the Ohio Valley.

St. Clair meant well. So did his men. But they were attacked by Little Turtle and a large force of Indians who fought furiously from behind trees and while lying on the ground. Cannon were useless against this type of warfare. St. Clair and his men were surrounded. The Indians picked off militiamen with deadly accuracy. They also killed General Butler of Pennsylvania, one of

159

St. Clair's chief officers. St. Clair, in desperation, ordered
a bayonet charge against the Indians in his rear, thus
clearing a route for a retreat. The Indians chased St. Clair's
men for four miles and then returned to gather up the
plunder.

Was Joseph Brant in this battle? One hundred and
fifty Mohawks fought there and members of Brant's
family claimed in later years that he had been present.
The Mohawk Chief never supplied the answer.

As a matter of fact, Brant's movements during the ten
years following the close of the war were full of mys-
tery. He would disappear for months at a time and
suddenly reappear dramatically at some council or battle.

General Knox, American Secretary of War, invited him
to a great council in Philadelphia. Brant wrote Knox that
he did not intend to parade through the streets of
Philadelphia with a motley group of chiefs.

Knox wrote again on behalf of President Washington,
"He considers your mind more enlightened than theirs
(the Indians), and he hopes that your heart is filled with
a true desire to serve the essential interests of your
countrymen. The United States is now fighting reluc-
tantly. To bring the fighting to a conclusion must result
in utter destruction of hostile Indians. We are desirous,
for the sake of humanity, of avoiding such a catas-
trophe."

Brant agreed to come to Philadelphia, but wrote that
he had to dispatch messengers to the Western Indians to
get their opinion before making the trip. When the great
council was held in April, 1792, he did not show up.

War clouds were rising fast. General Anthony Wayne,
known to the Indians as The Black Snake, was preparing
to invade the Ohio country with a large army and thus
settle the Indian question by force. The British, realizing
that such an invasion would drive them from Niagara,
asked Brant to stem the tide. The American Commissioners appeared at Niagara and were escorted to a council at the Detroit River. Brant tried to have the British

come as mediators, but they refused. The Western Indians proposed that the old boundary established by the Treaty of Fort Stanwix be kept. The Commissioners came back with an offer to the Indians of a large annual sum of money as a substitute for the loss of their lands.

Joseph Brant's reply to the Commissioners was probably the greatest speech of his career. It was a wonderful defense of the rights of the Indians to their land.

"Brothers," he told the Commissioners, "we are of the same opinion as the people of the United States. You consider yourselves an independent people. We are the original inhabitants of this country and sovereigns of the soil, and look upon ourselves as equally independent and free as the other nations. This country was given to us by the Great Spirit above and we wish to enjoy it.

"Brothers. We will not sell our lands under any consideration. Money is of no value to Indians. The white settlers are poor. Why don't you divide among them the money you would give to us and leave us with our lands?

"Brothers. You have talked to us of concessions. It appears strange that you expect any from us, who have only been defending our just rights against invasion. We want peace. Restore to us our country and we shall be enemies no longer.

"Brothers. We desire you to consider that our only demand is the peaceable possession of a small part of our once great country. Look back and view the lands from whence we have been driven to this spot. We can retreat no further, because the country behind us hardly affords food for its present inhabitants; and we have therefore resolved to leave our bones in this small space to which we are now consigned."

The Commissioners returned home without giving way an inch. General Wayne marched into the Ohio country. Little Turtle and his Indians attacked him at Fort Recovery and were mowed down by the cannon. The redskins removed their dead under cover of fog and night

and tried again the next day—with the same result.
Wayne chased them toward the Rapids of the Miami,
where the British had erected a fort. Here he caught up
with Little Turtle and completely routed him. The
British, safely behind the walls of the fort, did not admit
the fleeing Indians, but merely watched them being massacred. The Indians, convinced that the British no longer
planned to help them in their struggle against the United
States, signed the Treaty of Greenville, which drove them
out of most of the Ohio country.

Joseph Brant played no part in this decisive battle and
treaty for he lay dangerously ill at his home in Grand
River. The few Mohawks who left Grand River to fight
came back with the following message from the Western
Indians:

"You Mohawk Chief! What are you doing? Time was
when you roused us to war and told us that if all the
Indians would join the King, they should be a happy
people and become independent. In a very short time
you changed your voice and went to sleep and left us in
the lurch. You Mohawk Chief! You have ruined us and
you shall share with us. Know it is not good for you to
lie still any longer. Arise and bestir yourself!"

Brant's attitude toward the British at this time is best
expressed in a letter written several years later to his old
friend and playmate, Sir John Johnson.

"In the first place," Brant wrote, "the Indians were
engaged in a war to assist the English—then left in the
lurch at the peace to fight alone until they could make
peace for themselves. After repeatedly defeating the
armies of the United States so that *they* sent commissioners to endeavor to get peace, the Indians were so
advised as prevented them from listening to any terms
and hopes were given to them of assistance. A fort was
even built in their country, under the pretense of giving
refuge in case of necessity; but when that time came, the
gates were shut against them as enemies. They were
doubly injured by this, because they relied on it for

support, and were deceived. Were it not for this reliance on mutual support, their conduct would have been different."

Chapter XXIX

"My Roots Are No Longer Here."

THE Mohawk Chief was filled with homesickness for the land of his youth. Friends advised him against travelling through a section where mothers lulled children to sleep by whispering, "Hush, or Joseph Brant will come and scalp you." He ignored this advice and set out with two white companions and two Indian servants.

It was the Moon of Strawberries. The warm breath of Orenda caused the treetops to whisper a welcome. Birds hopped from limb to limb to tell him he was going home. Squirrels flicked their brushes and gossiped about him as they scampered up and down the trunks on important errands. All nature seemed to rejoice at his approach.

And Joseph's heart beat in tune with his surroundings. He became a small boy again in spirit, paddling down the Mohawk River in his bark canoe, swimming in its silvery water. He paused before a sturdy beech and examined its bark.

"I know this place well," he told his companions. "It was here I used to hide my paddle so that the other boys could not steal it. I would bend this tree down, tie my paddle to its tip, and then let the tree swing back in place. Then when I wanted my paddle I would climb the tree, bend it down again and get my paddle."

"On that large tree?" asked one of his companions.

"That was—let me see—forty years ago. It was a sapling then. I put my mark on it. See?"

And, sure enough, the wound the boy Thayendanegea had made on the bark was still visible.

164

"I too was a sapling," he said, his voice filled with remembrance of the past. "My roots were planted in the finest soil in all this land. I grew up here like this tree. But my roots are no longer here. They have been torn up by hands which did not love the Indian. Come, let us go on."

Night was drawing its blanket over the sun as the party rode into Canajoharie, where they planned to spend the night. The Mohawk Chief was dressed in the costume of the Pale Face. He looked much like some western settler travelling toward Albany and New York. He followed his companions into the inn and was shown to a room. He did not notice that the innkeeper stared hard at him and turned pale.

The evening was spent at the home of Major Robert Cochran, once among the gallant defenders of Fort Stanwix and since the war one of Brant's best friends. They talked over old times and also gave some attention to the Indian problem. It was late when Cochran accompanied Brant toward his lodging place.

The inn was ablaze with lights and a crowd had gathered nearby. Angry voices could be heard as men discussed some matter of importance. Cochran placed a hand on Brant's arm. From the shadows came one of Brant's travelling companions.

"What is it?" asked Cochran.

"Those fellers are out to make trouble. The Innkeeper recognized Captain Brant and he's told every man in the village. I think you'd better stay away from the inn, Captain."

"But why?" asked Brant. "I have paid for my room at the inn. I am entitled to go there."

"Those men might make things uncomfortable for you," said Cochran. "Your reputation around here isn't too good."

"But the war has been over for more than ten years," Brant protested.

"I'm sorry, but it won't be over for you during your

lifetime, my friend. Come, we'll go over to Schuyler's. No one would dare to attack you there. Your friends can bring your things along. And I would advise that you leave Canajoharie early in the morning."

Brant rose to his full height. "I am no coward," he cried. "I count my deaths as the great eagle numbers his feathers in the morning sun."

"It isn't a case of cowardice, Captain. It is a matter of good judgment."

"Very well. I shall do as you say."

The Mohawk Chief stayed with the Schuylers that night but he slept little. Not that he was thinking of the men at the inn, for he had no fear of them. His mind was too full of pictures of days long departed. He saw in memory the bark hut of Nickus Brant. He recalled his mother and his first wife, both dead these many years. He played again at deer buttons with William of Canajoharie, whose bones were part of the ravine at Oriskany. He chased snowshoe rabbits in the balsam swamps and hunted deer across the river. And ever recurring before him were the heroes of his boyhood, King Hendrick and Sir William Johnson. He wondered what they would think of him. Would they feel that he had fought a good fight in the interests of his people? Had he been a real leader?

He rose and went to the window. The Strawberry Moon was a yellow powder horn in the starlit sky. A lonely frog croaked to its mate from the swamp beside the river. He called again, but no answer came. And a great lump rose to the throat of Joseph Thayendanegea. For he knew that all these things were lost to him forever.

The party rode south to Philadelphia, where Brant was received by President Washington and Secretary Knox. The conference was satisfactory. Brant promised to make a peace mission to the Western Indians.

The return was through New York, which city he had not seen since those days in 1776 when he had entered it with Lord Howe's victorious army after the Battle of Long Island. He stayed at the Province Arms on Broadway near Trinity Church. Here he was entertained at dinner by Morgan Lewis, who brought with him a guest.

"Captain Brant," said Lewis, "I would like to have you meet your old rival, Colonel Marinus Willett."

Brant hesitated. He surveyed from head to foot the tall gentleman who was holding out a hand. Here was the hook-nosed, grizzled New Yorker whose military skill had spelled defeat and ruin for the Tories and Indians in the Mohawk Valley. Here was the man who had destroyed the Indian camp before Fort Stanwix and had been nicknamed "The Devil" by the Iroquois. Now Willett was known as a friend to all Indians. Brant accepted his hand.

"I welcome you to my old home," said Willett.

"Your home?"

Willett laughed. "I lived here in the Province Arms as a boy, Captain Brant. My father once kept this inn. That was long ago, before the war. My father was a Tory, as you may have heard."

"And you fought on the other side?"

"Gladly."

"That is something a Mohawk could not do. We fought with the British because our forefathers had made covenants with the King and we considered those covenants a sacred thing. But I shall forgive you, Colonel Willett, for a little bird has told me that you visited the Creeks and the Cherokees two summers ago and made their council fires burn brightly."

"Thank you, Captain. I feel it is my duty to do everything in my power to bring peace between your people and mine."

The conversation carried on for some time. It was interrupted by a commotion in the taproom. The proprietor of the inn came up to Colonel Willett.

"There's a man out there who says his name is Dygert. He comes from somewhere in the Mohawk Valley. He wants to kill Captain Brant."

Brant's face flushed. "Then why doesn't he come and do it?" he snapped.

Colonel Willett rose and left the room. His conversation with Dygert could be overheard by Brant and Lewis.

"What is your business?" Willett asked Dygert.

"I'm here to kill a damned Indian."

"Do you know that if you kill an Indian you will be hanged?"

"Who would hang me for killing an Indian?"

"You will see. I happen to be High Sheriff of this city and county. If you kill this Indian you may depend upon it that you will be hanged immediately."

Dygert thought the matter over. "Very well," he answered at last, "if that be the law, I'll give up the idea and go home. But I never heard you couldn't kill an Indian anywhere."

Willett returned. "I'm sorry you were disturbed, Captain," he said by way of apology.

"So am I," Brant admitted, "but evidently I must expect such things." He told of his experience at Canajoharie. "What was once my home is mine no longer."

Chapter XXX

"Have Pity on the Poor Indians."

THE Mohawk settlement at Grand River became Joseph Brant's chief concern. To it had come not only the Mohawks of the Upper Castle but also Indians from other Iroquois nations. White men, particularly Loyalists who had lost all in the war, began to settle Brant's land. The Chief saw that the hunting grounds of his people would soon be used up. To pay for the loss of game, he encouraged agriculture among his people. He also sold plots of land. With this money he built a school and a church.

Joseph was proud of the church, which was made of squared logs, boarded on the outside, and painted. In the belfry hunt a brass bell. The interior was furnished with a pulpit, a reading desk, a communion table, and comfortable pews. A small organ provided music.

To this new church Brant invited his old friend John Stuart as rector. Stuart was unable to accept the appointment, but he journeyed from Kingston to preach a Sunday service, baptize sixty-five Indians and marry three couples. The preacher brought with him half of the silver plate from the Indian chapel at Fort Hunter. The remaining portion he gave to Deseronto's colony at the Bay of Quinte.

Once the news of Brant's land sales reached Quebec, the British government protested. It not only forbade him from selling lands, but tried to strip him of half his possessions. Brant produced Haldimand's deed and saved Grand River for the Mohawks. He was angered by this

169

attempt to rob the Mohawks of their land. He wrote to Sir John Johnson as follows:

"You know we demand nothing new. We have no demand for compensation of our hunting grounds, which were very extensive, nor for our wood-lands adjoining our improvements. All we ask is a confirmation of our just right to this very land, which we receied in place of those for which we received no compensation. I presume few loyalists have omitted charging, or receiving pay for their woodlands, as we did; many of whom received lands who had never possessed one foot before."

He sent his nephew, John Norton, to England to place the case of the Indians before Lord Dorchester.

Despite his difficulties over land matters, Brant's life at Grand River would have been happy if it had not been for the waywardness of his son, Isaac. That young man had never loved his father. He now showed an intense jealousy of Brant's third wife, Catharine, and her seven children. Isaac felt that he was being treated unfairly, though he did nothing himself to deserve any special favors.

Captain Brant thought that if Isaac were married he might reform, so he arranged the wedding of his eldest son to the beautiful daughter of a Mohawk chief of the Tortoise clan. He also made Isaac his secretary and took him along to councils and conferences. Isaac used these occasions for getting drunk and starting fights. When under the influence of fire water, his favorite amusement was insulting his father and threatening his life.

Despite protests from his father, Isaac began to take matters into his own hands. One night, while drunk, he attacked a young man on the highway, shot his horse from under him, and badly maimed his victim. To prevent imprisonment for Isaac, Brant paid a heavy fine.

Some time later Isaac walked into the harness shop of a man named Lowell and said, "Lowell, I'm going to kill you."

The harnessmaker, knowing Isaac was drunk, laughed and asked, "Why should you kill me, Isaac?"

"I'm going to kill you," repeated Isaac, drawing his pistol.

Lowell became alarmed. "I have never injured you," he cried, "nor have we even quarreled."

Isaac pulled the trigger. Lowell slumped to the floor, dead.

The news reached Captain Brant as he was planning to leave for a council on Lake Champlain. He went to Isaac's house, sobered him up, and took him away from Grand River.

Isaac hardly spoke to his father during the long journey. At Burlington Heights, he spent his time in the taproom of a tavern while his father arranged with Colonel Beasley for the annual bounty of presents of clothing and other articles.

Brant returned to the inn, tired after the day's dealings. He slumped into a chair before the fire. From the taproom rose the sound of a familiar voice. It was Isaac, in the cups, attacking his father's reputation with falsehoods and dirty talk.

There is a limit to any man's endurance and Joseph Brant had strained his beyond the breaking point. He rose from his chair and walked into the taproom.

Isaac was sitting at a table airing his opinions before a group that showed its disgust at his performance. Isaac saw his father! He rose to his feet, swaying unsteadily. "There he is, the old—" a stream of profanity finished the sentence.

Joseph Brant stared at his son. He said nothing.

Isaac drew a dagger from his belt and rushed at his father. Captain Brant's hand grasped the hilt of the dirk he carried at his side. The downward stroke of Isaac's weapon missed the father's chest and wounded his hand.

Joseph Brant saw red. Losing all control of himself, he raised his dirk and struck blindly at his son. The blade slashed Isaac across the head. It cut through his hat and wounded his scalp. The force of the blow knocked him down.

Hands seized Brant's arms and pinned them to his side. There was no need for that, for the Mohawk Chief had regained his senses. On the floor before him lay his eldest son. His head was bleeding from a wound that had been inflicted by his own father.

"Get some water and some cloth," said Joseph Brant.

A doctor appeared to examine the wound. "It's only a surface cut," he said. "He'll recover in a few days if he keeps the bandages on." He cleaned the wound and bandaged Isaac's head. The wounded man, in a drunken stupor, was put to bed.

Isaac reappeared later in the night in the taproom. He had torn off the bandage. His head was bleeding afresh. He was taken back to his room and tied to his bed. The next day he escaped and continued his drinking. That evening he came down with brain fever. He died several days later.

Joseph Brant surrendered to the civil authorities and resigned his commission in the British service. The courts judged him not guilty of murdering his son and his resignation was not accepted. The Mohawk Chief returned to Grand River to place his case before a council of the sachems.

After talking the matter over, the sachems replied, "Brother, we have heard and considered your case. We sympathize with you. You are bereaved of a beloved son. But that son raised his parricidal hand against the kindest of fathers. His death was occasioned by his own crime. With one voice we acquit you of all blame. We tender you our hearty condolence. And may the Great Spirit above bestow upon you consolation and comfort under your affliction."

Joseph Brant never recovered from the horror of that night in the taproom. He would lie awake hour after hour, trying to discover ways in which the struggle could have been avoided. Isaac's death had much to do with shortening his life.

Brant's third wife became a source of comfort during

those trying years. Catharine was much younger than Joseph. She was a tall, straight woman, who was jolly and good-natured. To get Joseph's mind off his son's death, she encouraged him to introduce sports for the Indians.

The Senecas were invited to come to Grand River for an Indian ball play. Most of the Seneca nation appeared, either to take part in the game or to lay bets. The sides lined up and the stakes were placed on the ground in piles. The game had hardly started when a Mohawk player, in a sharp struggle for the ball with a Seneca, struck the latter in the face with his fist. The Senecas to a man dropped their sticks and retired into a sullen group. After a short conference they picked up their stakes and left for home.

Red Jacket and Cornplanter sent a delegation to Grand River to demand an apology. The Mohawks, much worried, asked for a council. Red Jacket and Cornplanter both came. Red Jacket made several fiery speeches, but Cornplanter agreed with Brant that they should smoke the calumet and try another play.

One thousand Senecas came to Grand River the following summer. The stakes in rifles, hatchets, swords, belts, knives, blankets, wampum, watches, beads, and furs were worth about one thousand dollars a side. A group of old chiefs sat beside the stakes to guard them during the play.

The game played was what is now called lacrosse. Each team consisted of 600 players, though only sixty took part on each side during actual play. When all was ready, a beautiful maiden, richly dressed in native costume including bracelets and a red tiara plumed with eagles' feathers, bounded gracefully into the center of the group of players and tossed the deerhide covered ball high into the air. Two warriors struggled to capture the ball in their rackets so they could hurl it toward their opponents' goal. The game was on! New players replaced wilted ones every fifteen minutes. For three days the

contest raged up and down the field. At the close the
Senecas were declared the victors and they went home
with the spoils.

Joseph Brant also turned to his younger children. He
took them fishing and hunting. He listened to their yarns
of the forest and told them the legends of the Mohawk
people. The two oldest boys, Joseph and Jacob, were
sent to Dartmouth College, where Dr. John Wheelock
served as President of the institution which had been
founded by Joseph's old teacher, Eleazer Wheelock.

Brant's correspondence with Dr. Wheelock was both
frequent and intimate. In sending his boys to Dartmouth,
Brant wrote, "I would wish them to be studiously
attended to, not only as to their education, but likewise
as to their morals in particular." On another occasion he
wrote, "Nothing can ever efface from my memory the
persevering attention your revered father paid to my
education, when I was in the place my sons now are.
Though I was an unprofitable pupil in some respects, yet
my worldly affairs have been much benefited by the
instruction I have received. I hope my children may reap
better advantages under your care, both with respect to
their futures as well as their worldly welfare."

Red Jacket, the Seneca orator, had not forgiven Brant
and Cornplanter for calling him a coward during the
retreat of the Indians before the Blue Snake so many
years before. He had tried to ruin Cornplanter after the
Treaty of Fort Stanwix. That clever half-breed, by
branding Red Jacket as a witch, had nearly succeeded in
ousting the orator instead.

The talkative Seneca now decided to get Joseph Brant
removed as War Chief of the Iroquois Confederacy. His
council at Buffalo Creek was attended mostly by minor
chiefs and warriors. Red Jacket told the council that
Brant had been using Iroquois money to pay his own
travelling expenses. He also pointed out that the trip of
John Norton to England, though made at the expense of
the Indians, had been a total failure. He hinted also that

Brant had built a new home out of Mohawk funds. The council was stirred up by Red Jacket's oratory. It voted to remove not only Joseph Brant but all Mohawks from office in the Confederacy.

When Brant heard of these developments, he called together the Mohawks and addressed them at length. He offered to pay out of his own purse all moneys he had expended for public uses.

"My only crime," he said in closing, "is that I want to make you a happy people and for you to be able to call your land your own forever and not leave it doubtful whether it is yours or not . . . . Still you would almost brand me with the name of thief, although not one of you ever paid a penny to pay my expenses when I traveled on your public business . . . . I have used only the interest on the money to defray expenses. The principal has not been touched. And as for the false statement that I built my home with your money, that is the cruellest thing you could say of me."

The Iroquois met in council at Niagara to discuss Brant's case. Red Jacket, seeing the way the wind was blowing, stayed away. Brant was cleared of all charges and retained as War Chief of the Iroquois Confederacy.

He spent his last years in the new house he had built near the head of Lake Erie. Though suffering from an incurable disease which caused him untold pain, he carried on his business affairs and continued to make improvements in his settlement. Many things would have to be left undone. The history of his people, which he had begun to write so enthusiastically years before, would never be completed. His translation of the New Testament had ended with the Book of Mark. Further translations were in the hands of his nephew, John Norton, who was working on the Book of John. Other minds would have to carry on plans for a new union of all the Indians.

Joseph Thayendanegea had spent a lifetime working for his people. He had led them in war. He had tried to

lead them in peace. The road had been long and difficult. Much of his labors had been in vain. He knew now
that he had fought a losing struggle against overwhelming
odds. But he also was confident that he had never for a
moment ceased in his efforts to improve the condition of
his people.

He sat in his chair before a window overlooking the
lake which separated him from the land of his boyhood.
Calling to him his favorite nephew, he said, "John, I am
nearly sixty-five years old. I am ill. I shall not be here
much longer. Listen to me, John. Have pity on the poor
Indians. If you can get any influence with the great,
endeavor to do them all the good you can."